BRAVER
Than I Knew

By Cathy McCoy Collier

CREATIVE MINDS PUBLICATIONS

ISBN: 979-8-218-86251-0

Printed in the United States

To all the women over 50 starting over and creating something new: you are not alone, you are seen, you are always enough, and we'll find our brand-new morning together.

Table of Contents

Using this Book

This journal is written in 52 weeks. There are 4 pages per week and there are 7 activities for the week. The weeks are essentially the same, however, I alternate between two designs for the last page of the week: one week will be "How are you feeling today?" and the next week "What are you grateful for this week?

I designed the book so you can choose to do one quick, activity a day. However, you can make it your own. It is your journal, and it should reflect your path. Choose weeks with themes that are what you need.

Although I use the word "divorce" about my path, it could be used for any ending of a relationship. Whether it is a partnership, a break-up or an annulment, I hope my book helps you navigate your new life.

Page 1 of the week:

Section 1 or Sunday – My Story. I will share my story based on a theme of the week. These are my experiences, but they are certainly not unique to me. I am hoping to show you are not alone.

I'll explain why this week was important to me or why this week felt like a necessary, but sometimes painful, step in the right direction.

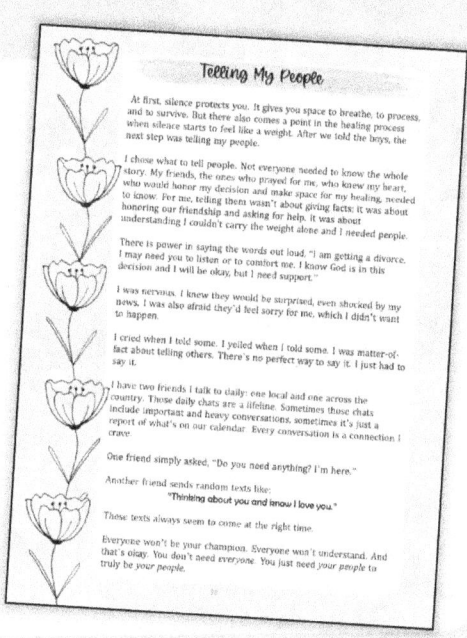

Page 2 of the week:

Section 2 or Monday – Bible Verse. I have selected a bible verse to correspond with my theme of the week.

Section 3 or Tuesday - Coloring Page. I have included a picture coloring. One thing I have found comfort in is the mindless task of coloring. I purchased adult coloring books and markers and hit the pause button to breathe while I did this. That is my hope for you.

Page 3 of the week:

Section 4 or Wednesday –Song. I am a song person. Music and songs are closely connected to most of my core memories. During my separation and divorce, music became vitally important. I have chosen a song that is connected to the theme of the week. Check it out on your preferred music platform.

Section 5 or Thursday – Reflection Questions. Each week there are 3 questions to help you put your thoughts into words. Sometimes the sheer act of writing it down, makes it better.

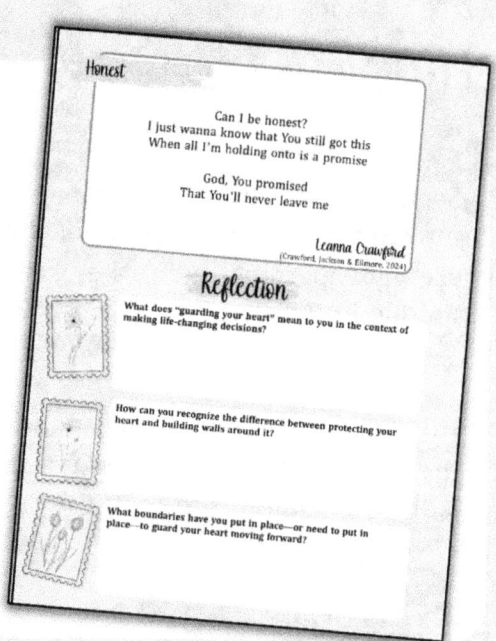

Page 4 every other week:

Section 6 or Friday – How do you feel? This time in our lives is steeped with emotions. Take a minute and jot them down. Document how you are feeling and allow yourself to feel everything. Use the box to jot a date, a time, or color a feeling (maybe red for anger, yellow for peace).

Section 7 or Saturday – Prayer of the Week. This prayer will reflect the Sunday meditation. If possible, speak it out loud. It also doesn't need to be saved for the end of the week...it can be used as a daily affirmation.

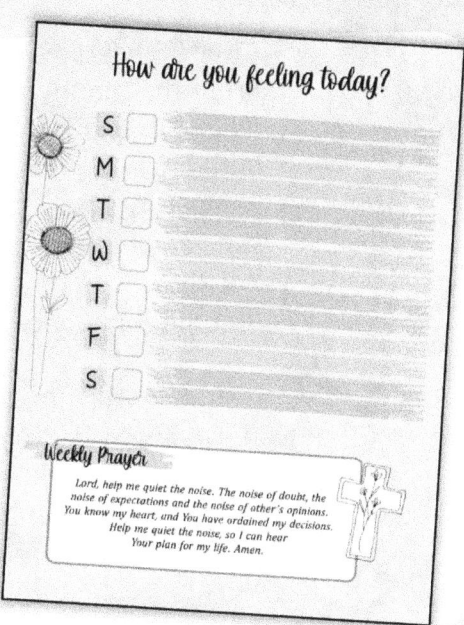

Page 4 every other week:

Section 6 or Friday – What are you grateful for this week? It is very easy to get weighed down by all the emotions and get lost in the desperation.

Make sure you are taking time for all the things in your life that are good and be grateful.

Nothing is too small to go on these lines. Try to fill each line each week.

Introducing Myself

After 32 years of marriage, I reached my limit—I knew I had to leave. From that moment on, my freedom was non-negotiable. Even though I felt weak and powerless, a quiet voice told me otherwise. I clung to my faith knowing that I deserved better. I knew I wasn't the first woman to start over at fifty-eight or the first to reach her breaking point and say, "enough." I wasn't the first to long for someone who understood exactly what I was going through—but it certainly felt like I was the first and only one.

Instead of turning to books about divorce, I turned to scripture and journaling. I had written a professional book about teaching reading and created workbooks for early learners, but this time I wanted to create the journal I had searched for and couldn't find. A journal for women like me—no custody battles, no celebrity platforms, just real life, and real emotions. A space for women in their fifties who are starting over and rediscovering who they are beyond being a wife and a mother. In these pages, I write honestly and vulnerably, sharing both the highs and lows of my journey. My hope is that through my story, you'll find comfort, strength, and the reminder that you are never truly alone.

In 1992, I promised to love, honor and cherish; I thought my happily ever after had arrived. I didn't necessarily think our lives would be easy, because life isn't always easy, but I thought that special day meant I had a partner through it all. I was twenty-five years old, and we began to build a family.

I have two sons, and they have always made me proud. They were good students, good friends, and respectful young men. I've loved being their mom every single day, not just on the fun days, but on the real ones too. We spent most of their childhood on the soccer field (and they are still playing on soccer teams twenty-five years later). Their father was their first coach. I was jealous of the special connection my boys had with their dad through soccer.

My relationship with them was different. I was the "heavy" in our family. Although I was on the sidelines for soccer every weekend, I was the bad cop to their dad's good cop at home. I was the disciplinarian, and it felt like he was "Father of the Year." My ex and I would have discussions in private about enforcing rules as a team, but it rarely happened that way.

It wasn't until one son was in college and one preparing to leave that I finally had the proof that confirmed suspicions I had for a year: my then husband was having an affair. I was heartbroken. However, at the time I decided I would be willing to stay if we went to a counselor. I wanted to stay for my sons. I was willing to stay because of the vows I made in front of God, for better or for worse. I was also willing to stay for financial reasons, and he chose to stay.

We went to a Christian marriage counselor, hoping to repair what had been broken. I wanted to understand how we got there and if it could be fixed. But week after week, the focus seemed to land on me—what I needed to change and what I could do differently. I left feeling unseen, unheard, and confused. He was the one who betrayed our vows, yet somehow, I was the one expected to do the work. After several sessions and countless late-night talks, we promised to communicate better and fight for our marriage. I already knew words wouldn't be enough; I wanted to see actions – his actions.

Not much time passed before he cheated a second time. I cried. He apologized, but then he did it again. These weren't affairs built on love or even connection; they were brief encounters and careless choices. But betrayal doesn't have to last long to break something inside you.

In 2024, I discovered evidence that finally brought me to my limit. I was finished. I cried for hours. I took off my wedding ring and never put it back on. I decided that day we would be getting a divorce. The next few weeks were a blur. I was determined we both sit down with our sons and tell them what was happening at the same time. They deserved to know before anyone else. Telling my sons was one of the hardest things I've ever been a part of.

Although I knew getting divorced was the right decision, it didn't mean it was easy. At the time, we didn't tell them everything. I wanted them to maintain their relationship with their father. There were so many emotions to navigate. First, it's embarrassing! Who wants people to find out that your husband didn't see enough in you, so he looked elsewhere? Not me. If I could fix my marriage, no one would have to know, right? I wouldn't have to tell anyone. But, when he cheats over and over, it becomes even more embarrassing to admit that you didn't leave after the first time.

Second, it's scary. There were so many unanswered questions. Where would I live? How would I tell my family? I have never been in charge of paying bills. *Could I manage finances?* Could I be on my own? I had never even lived alone. What would that be like? What would holidays look like? How would this affect not just family, but our friends? It was all terrifying.

At some point, I began to recognize each time he cheated, and I stayed, I shrank. I became less "me." I had stopped expressing my thoughts or making waves, hoping I could be enough. But you can't find peace if you are on constantly on guard. I realized I had been on guard for ten years.

After my decision was made, the process began and I felt like I was trying to reclaim myself. I began to examine my relationship with God. I was raised in the church, but my relationship with God seemed to be smaller. I wasn't attending church regularly because I was probably a little mad at Him. I was a "good person." Why was I dealing with this bad stuff? Since a Christian counselor made me feel like the problem, I began to wonder if God thought I was the problem. Admittedly, I felt like I turned my back on God, but He hadn't abandoned me. He was continuing to work behind the scenes for my good.

In retrospect, His work began before I even made any decisions. A few months before I left, a dear friend confided in me at lunch that he had been sent separation papers from his wife's lawyer. He needed a friend, someone to listen and offer support. Not only did I listen, but I also learned about divorce from a legal standpoint, not knowing I'd personally need this information in the months to come.

Days before my decision to leave, I read Colleen Hoover's, *It Ends with Us.* I didn't like the negative press it was getting, and I knew a book about domestic violence would be heavy, but a friend gave it to me. She wanted us to see the movie the following Saturday. I got the book on Wednesday and Thursday night while lying in bed, I read the words, "We all have a limit."

In the book, the mother discusses "her limit" for three paragraphs. I read those paragraphs without taking a breath. She described staying in a marriage that was unsafe but feeling like she was doing it for a reason. I felt the weight of her words immediately. Although I was not a victim of domestic violence, I related to her explanation of reaching your limit. I felt exposed. I quietly gathered myself, finished the book, and rolled over for the night. My ex said, "Wow, you read that book fast, you must have liked it." I remember saying to him, "That was the most intensely sad book I've ever read, and I can't talk about it yet."

Then, hours before I found the evidence that would end my marriage, I was sitting in a restaurant and heard Matthew West's song, "Truth Be Told," coming through the speakers. The lyrics to the song talk about hiding true feelings because the world expects you to have it all together, even when you don't. Having that song on my mind that day helped me come to the conclusion that I no longer wanted to pretend things were ok.

Looking back, these three moments proved to me that God was present in my life and was preparing me for what would come next.

This journal is about what happened after my decision. It's about change. It's about growth. It's about being brave enough to want more for myself. It's about being brave enough to become myself again. A friend said to me, "Cath, this (divorce) is part of your story, but it isn't your whole story." He was right. This is about my fresh start in the middle of my story.

From the first day I told my parents, my mom repeatedly told me, "I'm so proud of you. You're so brave." At the time I felt anything but brave. Brave would have left long ago. While talking with my cousin about not feeling brave, she reassured me. "You are brave. Even when you didn't have answers, you left. Even when you were terrified about money, you left. Even when you didn't know what it would look like for your family, you left. Stop and give yourself credit. You are brave." They helped me see I was braver than I knew.

Knowing My Limit

Like I said in the introduction, "We all have a limit." It's a good thing. Our limit can guide us to being authentic. Getting there isn't fun, though.

Previously I knew I *should* be at my limit. While I was hurt and understood no one deserved to be treated with such disrespect, I was too afraid to make a move. But this time, even with unanswered questions hanging in the air, I knew I was done. I knew I could not be in this relationship anymore.

I started immediately making plans for what was next. My limit was about taking control!

I decided I wouldn't move out or kick him out while I was looking for a new home. In Virginia, you can be "separated while living together" if certain boundaries are set. Those boundaries were quickly and firmly set. I also declared my Limit Day as the official date of separation, and he agreed to it. That being said, I want to stress I never felt unsafe around him or in the house. Your safety should never be compromised. Check with the laws in your state for details.

What did I want from this divorce? I wanted to stop wondering. I wanted to stop being paranoid and waiting for the next shoe to drop because I knew it would. I wanted a new life where I was valued. I wanted to cultivate people who positively impacted my life. I remember looking in the mirror and asking myself if I would want my children, my sister, my nieces or my friends to accept this behavior in their partners. Obviously, I didn't want it for them, why would I want it for me?

I believe God knew I needed to be pushed to my limit before I would act.

Own your limit and move to a brighter day and a brand-new morning. 1 Corinthians assures us that God knows there is a limit to what we can bear, so don't be afraid to show it. 1 Corinthians also says He will help find a way forward.

> "And God is faithful; He will not let you be tempted beyond what you can bear. But when you are tempted, He will also provide a way out so that you can endure it."
>
> 1 Corinthians 10:13

Breakthrough

This is not a breakdown
It's a breakthrough
This is not a midnight
It's a brand-new morning
When it dawns on the dark
No, this is not the moment
When it all falls apart
It's a beautiful place to start.

Andrew Ripp

(Ripp, Rinehart, &Hulce, 2025)

Reflection

What moment made you realize you've hit your limit?

What does your "brighter day" or "brand new" feel like? Can you describe it in detail?

What does taking control look like for you right now—big or small?

How are you feeling today?

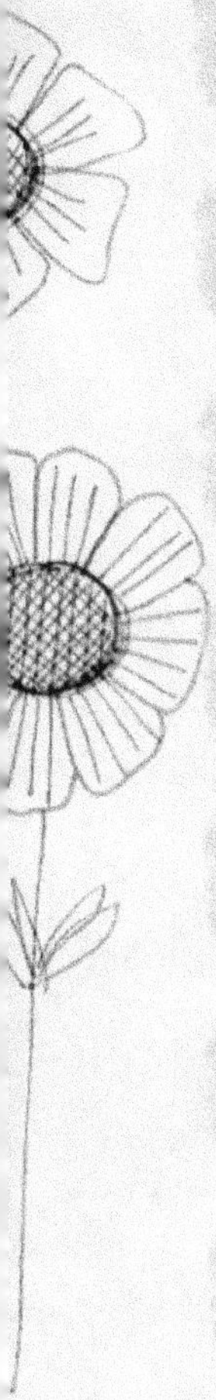

S ☐

M ☐

T ☐

W ☐

T ☐

F ☐

S ☐

Weekly Prayer

Lord, Thank You for showing me that my limits are not weaknesses but wisdom. When I reach the end of what I can bear, help me see it as Your signal to step forward in faith. Give me courage to trust that brighter days await in Your plan. Amen.

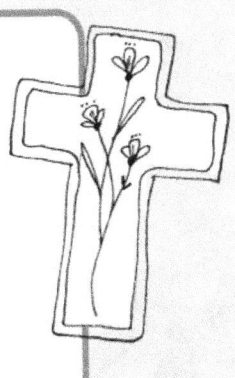

Guarding My Heart

I spent so much time pretending everything was fine. I wore a smile, made the excuses, and convinced myself that things might change. Honestly, things weren't always bad. We had fun times and beautiful moments. We celebrated special holidays and events in our family. Despite all those times, I would find myself wondering when it would happen again. I would look at the memories tab on social media and events would be tainted in retrospect because I knew behind the camera, I had just discovered another infidelity. I felt like I needed to protect my family from the ugliness. I thought protecting my family meant staying.

After the decision was made, I was left standing in unfamiliar territory – exposed and raw. Saying "no more," isn't about saying it once. It's understanding that I was saying "no more" to family holidays, family dinners, family movie nights, eating out together, and family game night. Ultimately, I was saying, "no more" to being a family.

The blame felt like it shifted from his actions to my actions. When we told the boys, I kept apologizing for breaking our family. I felt like I had done this *to* our family. In truth, his actions had consequences. His actions lead to my actions. I had been making decisions for the past 10 years to keep my family whole, but now I needed to make a decision for myself. It felt selfish.

In fact, it wasn't selfish. It as time and I needed to stand up for myself. I needed to recognize I deserved more. However, the ache of standing by a decision you never wanted to make but knew you had to for your own peace and well-being.

Did I have all the answers at this point? Absolutely, not. Did I even know all the questions to ask? Again, no. Did I know I was firm in my decision? YES.

Proverbs 4 reminds me to "guard my heart." I was trusting that God was with me in this decision and in the weeks and months to come. He would be by my side. He would light my path, and He would help me find all the answers.

> *"Above all else, guard your heart,*
> *for everything you do flows from it."*

Proverbs 4:23

Honest

Can I be honest?
I just wanna know that You still got this
When all I'm holding onto is a promise

God, You promised
That You'll never leave me

Leanna Crawford
(Crawford, Jackson & Ellmore, 2024)

Reflection

What does "guarding your heart" mean to you in the context of making life-changing decisions?

How can you recognize the difference between protecting your heart and building walls around it?

What boundaries have you put in place—or need to put in place—to guard your heart moving forward?

What are you grateful for this week?

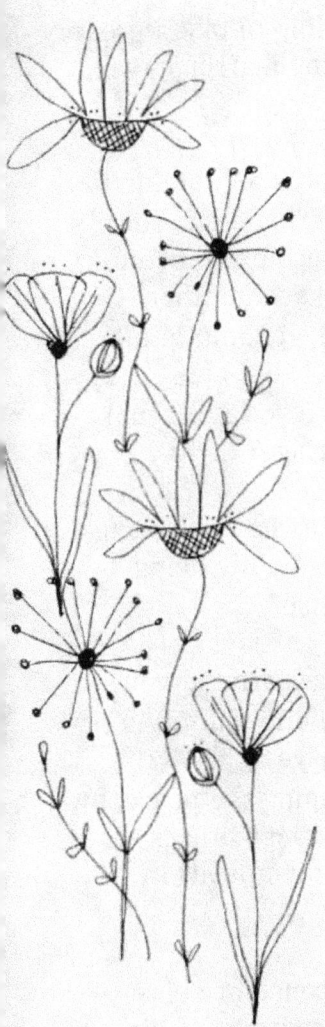

Weekly Prayer

Lord, help me guard my heart. Even though the decisions were hard, I know that You are in every decision. Help me be firm in my decisions while I navigate the unknown. I do know You will be there each step of the way. Amen.

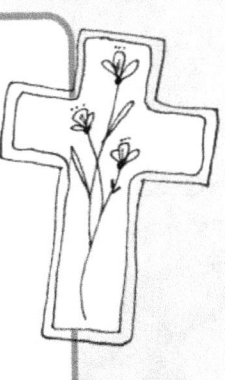

Quieting The Noise

Talking about quieting the noise is a funny thing for me to say. I am the original "Chatty Cathy." My high school teacher used me as an example for the vocabulary word loquacious ("tending to talk a great deal"). I'll talk to anyone, anytime, anywhere, but my marriage was different. I kept it to myself.

There is so much noise from the outside about what is acceptable in a marriage. It's frequently discussed on talk shows, podcasts, social media, television, and in movies. Infidelities have become comedic entertainment and important issues like how it makes the other partner feel "less than" are minimized or never talked about at all.

A dear friend asked me, "Are you sure? Are you sure you can't make this work? Are you sure you want to end your marriage?"

I know she was coming from a place of concern, but I had not been honest with myself for years. Now, I was sure. I was finally being honest with myself. Everyone's opinion was just noise.

Quieting the noise isn't just about silencing the voices around you - it's about learning to hear the voice within you, the one that often gets drowned out by the expectations of others. For years, I convinced myself I was doing the right thing by keeping the peace, by fixing what was broken, by living the version of marriage others said was acceptable. I became an expert at ignoring my own needs in favor of what looked right from the outside.

I have learned that you can't heal in the middle of constant noise. Quieting the noise means trusting yourself. It means sitting in silence long enough to know what you really need, what you can live with, and what you absolutely can't. The answer isn't out there or coming from someone else – it's in you. God is seeking the quietness to show you the path. And when you finally hear it, you'll know.

Philippians 4:8 says to think about what is true, noble, right, pure, lovely, admirable, excellent, or praiseworthy. God wants you to be all those things – for yourself. He wants your life to reflect those characteristics. He wants what's best for you. Don't worry about the noise.

"Finally, brothers and sisters, whatever is true, whatever is noble, whatever is right, whatever is pure, whatever is lovely, whatever is admirable — if anything is excellent or praiseworthy — think about such things."

Philippians 4:8

God, please help remind me of the things
I cannot see
When I'm broken down, defeated,
believing lies from the enemy
God, please help remind me of the day
death lost its sting
That I know You have a plan in the midst of suffering

Jet Trouble

(Troublefield, 2023)

Reflection

What are some examples of "noise" you've experienced from others when making difficult decisions?

What does it mean to *trust yourself* in the middle of a painful or life-changing situation?

Why do you think people (even those who love us) ask us to "make sure" about our decisions?

How are you feeling today?

S ☐

M ☐

T ☐

W ☐

T ☐

F ☐

S ☐

Weekly Prayer

Lord, help me quiet the noise. The noise of doubt, the noise of expectations and the noise of other's opinions. You know my heart, and You have ordained my decisions. Help me quiet the noise, so I can hear Your plan for my life. Amen.

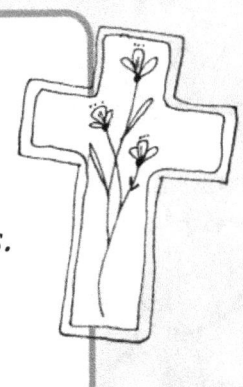

Making Lists

I am a list-maker. I like making a list and feeling accomplished as each item is checked off.

Proverbs 15:22 encourages us to seek counsel when making plans. That's hard. When you've been in a relationship where trust has been compromised or destroyed, it's difficult to reach out for help.

The People List – *Who do I tell? When? How? Who can I rely on? Who can I trust?* I made a list of close friends and family I needed to tell personally. I felt they needed to hear it from me.

The Money List –*What money was now mine to use for relocation? What income did I have? What was in checking, savings, investments, and annuities? What records could I access?* This was the biggest hurdle for me. My biggest anxiety about the divorce was money. When it comes to spousal support, retirement accounts, and everything money, it almost always becomes contentious. Make sure you have trusted counsel helping you navigate these waters.

The Housing List – *Where will I live that is safe and comfortable? What do I need? How will I furnish it?* I knew I wanted a condo because I didn't want to be responsible for a yard, but I had no idea what 1,700 square feet looked like. I also knew I wanted to stay in the same area. Thankfully, a sweet friend who was a real estate agent walked me through every step. She told me her daughter would be selling her condo in 6 months, and she thought it would be perfect but we both knew there was no way I could wait 6 months. She showed me several condo options in the next week. Then just one week later, God interceded. Incredulously, her daughter had put in a very low offer on a house and had gotten it. She needed to sell her condo as soon as possible. It was in the perfect location and had everything I wanted. God was there.

The Lawyer List – *What are the laws about separation and divorce in your state? Will it be fault or no-fault?* I contacted a lawyer early in the process. I kept a running list of questions on the Notes app on my phone.

Listen to Proverbs 15:22. Make the lists. Check the boxes. Seek counsel. In an uncertain time, check marks feel good.

> *"Plans fail for lack of counsel,
> but with many advisers they succeed."*
>
> Proverbs 15:22

Holy, there is no one like You
There is none beside You
Open up my eyes in wonder
And show me who You are
And fill me with Your heart
And lead me in Your love to those around me

Pat Barrett

(Redman, Martin, Kaple, Younker, & Barrett, 2018)

Reflection

What types of lists have helped you feel more in control during difficult seasons of life?

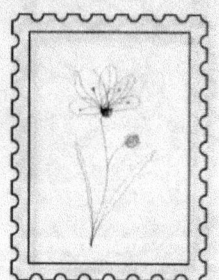

In what ways can making lists help bring clarity to emotional or overwhelming situations?

How does Proverbs 15:22 encourage you to invite God and others into your planning process?

What are you grateful for this week?

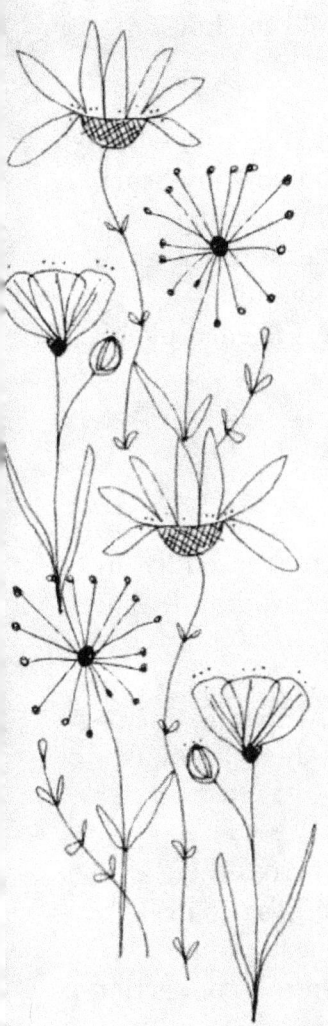

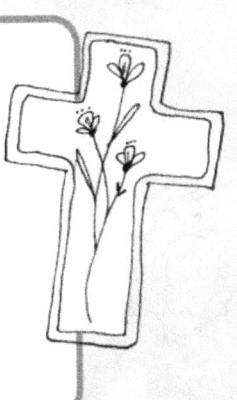

Weekly Prayer

God, You are the ultimate list maker. You make lists for my benefit and for my prosper. Thank You for Your plans and Your wisdom. Help me trust Your timing and Your guidance. Surround me with wise counsel, and give me courage to move forward, checking each step with You.
Amen.

Telling My People

At first, silence protects you. It gives you space to breathe, to process, and to survive. But there also comes a point in the healing process when silence starts to feel like a weight. After we told the boys, the next step was telling my people.

I chose what to tell people. Not everyone needed to know the whole story. My friends, the ones who prayed for me, who knew my heart, who would honor my decision and make space for my healing, needed to know. For me, telling them wasn't about giving facts; it was about honoring our friendship and asking for help. It was about understanding I couldn't carry the weight alone and I needed people.

There is power in saying the words out loud, "I am getting a divorce. I may need you to listen or to comfort me. I know God is in this decision and I will be okay, but I need support."

I was nervous. I knew they would be surprised, even shocked by my news. I was also afraid they'd feel sorry for me, which I didn't want to happen.

I cried when I told some. I yelled when I told some. I was matter-of-fact about telling others. There's no perfect way to say it. I just had to say it.

I have two friends I talk to daily: one local and one across the country. Those daily chats are a lifeline. Sometimes those chats include important and heavy conversations, sometimes it's just a report of what's on our calendar. Every conversation is a connection I crave, especially when living alone.

One friend simply asked, "Do you need anything? I'm here."

Another friend sends random texts like:
"Thinking about you and know I love you."

These texts always seem to come at the right time.

Everyone won't be your champion. Everyone won't understand. And that's okay. You don't need everyone. You just need your people to truly be your people.

> *"Let the redeemed of the Lord tell their story –*
> *those He redeemed from the hand of the foe."*
>
> Psalm 107:2

Wont' Start Now

Whatever comes
You've never let me walk alone
Not even once
And You won't start now

I'll never have to worry if I'll be alright
I'll never have to wonder if I'm on Your mind
I'll never see a breakthrough come that isn't right on time

Seph Schlueter
(Wedgeworth, Gamble & Schlueter, 2025)

Reflection

Who are your "people?"

What truth are you still learning to tell? Are there parts of your story you've avoided speaking aloud?

How does telling your story honor what God is doing in you?

How are you feeling today?

S

M

T

W

T

F

S

Weekly Prayer

Lord, help me tell my story to my people. In addition to You, I need people. I will need support in the form of listening ears, comforting hugs, and check-ins. Thank You for the people in my life who will be by my side. Amen.

Forgiving Myself

Forgiving myself. It sounds so simple, but it's one of the hardest things I've had to do.

I would never want anyone I love to accept the behavior I accepted for myself within my marriage. More than once, I had discovered an infidelity, cried with a broken heart, and allowed myself to be consoled. I also allowed myself to believe it would never happen again, while subconsciously I knew it might.

One of the first questions I asked my therapist was, "Why did I stay?" I thought I already knew the answer: I wasn't strong enough to walk away. But saying that out loud made me feel weak.

My therapist kindly told me to give myself grace. I didn't have all the information. Once I did, I found the strength and the courage to leave. Still, it felt like a consolation prize because I thought I should have been stronger all along.

When I talked to my brother-in-law about this, he also asked me why I stayed so long. Again, I confessed, I wasn't strong enough to leave. He was surprised. He told me I was one of the strongest people he knew. I'm good in a crisis, but it's different when you are fighting for someone else. You can look at things objectively and act accordingly; no emotions are necessary.

I felt like I had let myself down. I had my reasons for staying, but why hadn't I had one bold reason for leaving?

I've heard it said forgiving isn't about forgetting, it's about releasing your emotional connection to the event. If I could forgive myself, I could let go of the personal disappointment and truly move forward to heal. I don't think we should forget the actions, because it teaches us a lesson. But forgiveness is about letting it go so it doesn't dictate our reactions or compromise our future.

Just as Philippians says, I had to forget the past and move forward in His love. Part of healing is forgiving that scared, broken version of myself, the one who didn't know how to leave. God was ready to help me forgive myself and pave a path to new beginnings.

> *"Forgetting what is behind and straining toward what is ahead, I press on toward the goal to win the prize for which God has called me heavenward in Christ Jesus."*
>
> **Philippians 3:13-14**

All Because of Mercy

But the truth is I've been broken since my very first breath
And the truth is I've been wandering since my very first step

I know the only reason
I can stand here unashamed
Is not because I'm worthy
It's all because of mercy.

Casting Crowns
(Pruis, Hall, West 2022)

Reflection

Why is it often easier to be strong for others than it is to be strong for ourselves?

Knowing God is quick to forgive us when we ask for forgiveness, how can we be godlier about forgiveness?

What would you say to your past self to offer grace and compassion in that season of life?

What are you grateful for this week?

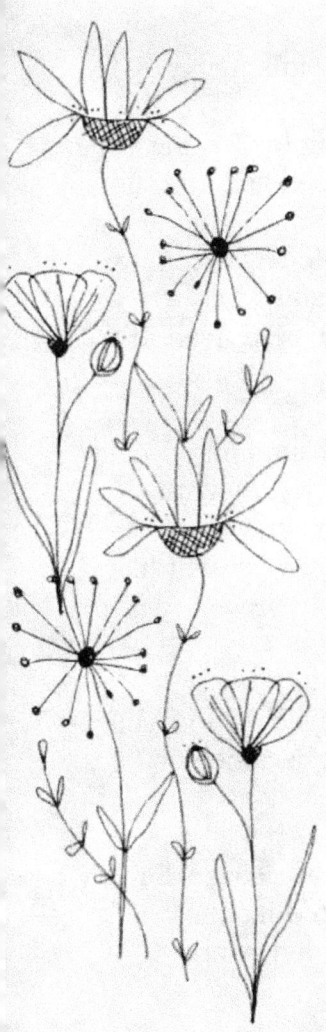

Weekly Prayer

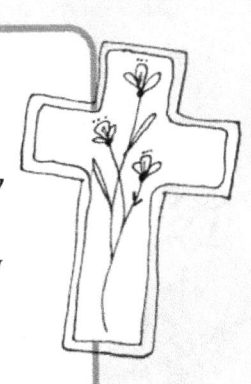

Lord, help me forgive the version of me who didn't know how to leave. Teach me to embrace healing, hope, and new beginnings, knowing You've already forgiven what I struggle to release. Amen.

Trusting His Timing

Before I had the courage to leave, it felt like staying was because of weakness.

Looking back now, I can see it differently—it was God's mercy.

Even though I didn't recognize it then, I was waiting for His perfect timing. The doors that needed to close weren't closed yet, and the strength I needed wasn't fully formed. God was preparing me in ways I didn't even realize. While I thought I was stuck, He was working behind the scenes, aligning circumstances, softening and strengthening my heart, and building the resolve I would need to move forward.

When the moment finally came, it wasn't because I suddenly decided I was brave. It was because God knew I was ready. He knew the exact day I would take my first step toward freedom, and He made sure I didn't take it a day too early or a day too late. What felt like delay was divine protection because on my Limit Day bravery was the only option at hand.

The exhaustion, the tears, the wondering if I'd ever feel like myself again – God met me in all of it. Each quiet moment became part of my preparation. Slowly, strength replaced survival.

Eventually, it wasn't just about leaving – it was about rising. There was a shift. I found energy I thought I'd lost. I started making decisions with clarity, setting boundaries with confidence, and walking forward without fear.

What once felt like crawling became walking. And what felt like walking has become something close to soaring.

That's what trusting His timing does. It strengthens you, restores you, and lifts you to places you couldn't reach on your own. I felt like I was drowning in disappointment and fear, but the truth is, I was never overcome. God was always there, holding me above the waves, carrying me forward until the right moment came and I could step out of the boat with confidence and strength. Braver than I knew.

His timing wasn't my timing – but it was perfect.

> *"In their hearts humans plan their course,*
> *but the Lord establishes their steps."*
>
> Proverbs 16:9

Always on Time

"I remember how You carried
When I couldn't take a step
And I remember how You loved me
When I couldn't love myself

Jesus
I was tossed in the water
But I never went under
You were always on time

Elevation Worship
(Furtick, Smith, Barrett, and Mooring, 2024)

Reflection

When have you felt "stuck," only to realize later that God was preparing you for something greater?

What is one thing about your journey that you know has been perfect in God's timing?

What steps are you taking next?

How are you feeling today?

S ☐

M ☐

T ☐

W ☐

T ☐

F ☐

S ☐

Weekly Prayer

God, I trust that Your timing is never late and always right. Help me wait with hope, rise with strength, and walk in faith—knowing you are guiding every step.
Amen.

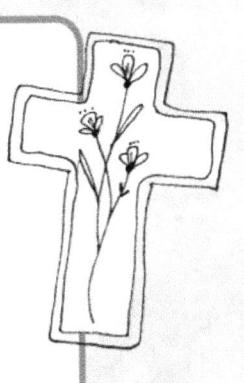

Decluttering: Stuff is Stuff

With Moving Day quickly approaching, it became necessary to divide everything we owned. I bought boxes on the way home from closing on my condo. I was ready to pack! As I walked through the house, I quickly realized there wasn't a lot I wanted to take with me. I wasn't going to take things I didn't need.

Too many "things" in that house seemed to be connected to the marriage. I suddenly wasn't interested in bringing these things into my new space. I began to realize that stuff is stuff. I didn't need a lot of stuff.

I wanted very specific things that meant something to me. I wanted pictures that my mom's friend had painted. I wanted specific figurines that meant something to me. I wanted the dining room set a good friend had given us when she moved and it was a connection to her. I wanted everything in my office. I wanted the Hope Chest my dad had refurbished and lined with cedar before I was married. I wanted the antique bedroom set I brought into the marriage 32 years before. I also wanted an antique croquet set. It meant something to me.

My condo was going to be about me. I wanted my own space created by me and for me and for my life moving forward.

Part of the divorce is moving on. I had a friend remind me that I will never get "justice" in the form of things or money. Things didn't hold us together. Things weren't going to change the fact that my marriage was ending.

Pictures and photo albums that documented my family, felt sad. I decided those pictures belong to my children and they should keep them as a memory of their childhood. I took some pictures of me with them, but I didn't take family pictures.

Just as Matthew 6 says don't worry about the things that can be stolen or taken but worry about your heart and your love and your faith. Things can be replaced but your peace of mind, your sense of worth, and your ability to love endlessly cannot.

Stuff is stuff and I didn't need it to move forward in His love.

"Do not store up for yourselves treasures on earth, where moths and vermin destroy, and where thieves break in and steal. But store up for yourselves treasures in heaven, where moths and vermin do not destroy, and where thieves do not break in and steal. For where your treasure is, there your heart will be also."

Matthew 6:19-21

Don't Stop Praying

He's close to the brokenhearted and
saves those who are crushed in spirit
The Alpha and Omega knows how your story ends
When you've cried,
and you've cried 'til your tears run dry

The answer won't come, and you don't know why
Don't Stop Praying

Matthew West
(West & Pardo, 2024)

Reflection

What items did you hold onto after your divorce, and why were they meaningful to you?

How can the act of physically decluttering help with emotional and spiritual healing?

Matthew 6:21 says, "For where your treasure is, there your heart will be also." What are you treasuring today, and how does that reflect where your heart is in this season?

What are you grateful for this week?

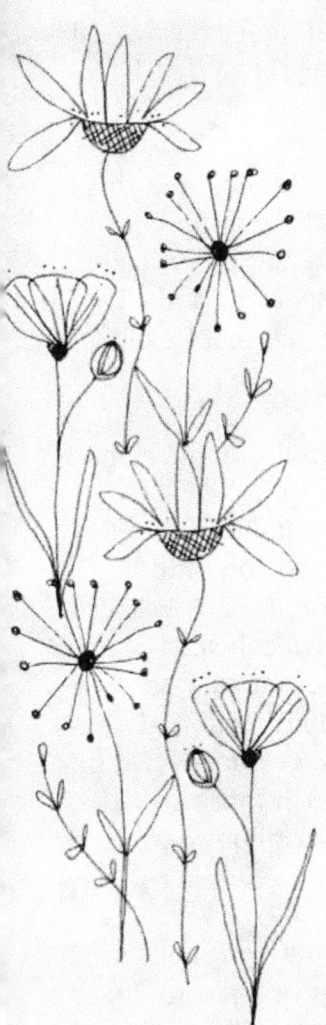

Weekly Prayer

Lord, help me release what no longer serves my heart or my future. Let me treasure what truly matters—faith, love, peace, and purpose. Remind me that things are temporary, but Your presence is eternal. Fill the empty spaces with hope and guide me as I build a life rooted in You. Amen.

Trusting Myself

This was a surprise to me. For thirty-two years, every decision I made was either made with my ex or in consideration of his opinions. When I started looking at condos, I had to figure out what I wanted, what I liked and make those decisions by myself. What I quickly realized is that I didn't know what I liked.

I had lived in the same house since 1995. We created a home in this house and over the years we made decisions about how to update and decorate. We made decisions about paint colors and bathroom tile and kitchen cabinets. Even when I acted spontaneously and stripped wallpaper in the foyer because I wanted it painted, I would always ask his opinion.

Suddenly everything was my choice, and I found myself floundering.

The condo I purchased had a black accent wall downstairs in the living room area. I never had anything painted black before and I didn't know what to do about it. I knew I could paint it, but I wasn't sure if I wanted to paint it. When I went looking for a couch, I showed my sister one that would work in a room with a painted black wall and one that would work in a room without a painted black wall. She liked them both but reminded me it was my decision. I decided to lean into the black wall and buy the couch that worked with it. My entire downstairs is now decorated in dark floors, gold accents and that black wall, and I love it!

Knowing what you like isn't just about decorating your new house. For me it was learning what to order at a restaurant or what to do on vacation. It was who I was without him. He had an opinion about everything. There were times I felt like he would second-guess my decisions or make me feel like I needed him to get it right. But the more decisions I made, I became empowered.

Learning what I liked without anyone else's opinions was equal parts exciting and scary. Sometimes finding your power is about making the first decision. I had already made the biggest one: starting over.

Since then, I have survived a million more decisions. Making decisions and relying on myself became easier. I also knew God was there with a spirit of power and love.

> *"For God has not given us a spirit of fear,*
> *but of power and of love*
> *and of a sound mind."*
>
> 2 Timothy 1:7

Even If

I know You're able and I know You can
Save through the fire with Your mighty hand

I know the sorrow, and I know the hurt
Would all go away if You'd just say the word
But even if You don't
My hope is You alone

Mercy Me

(Millard, Glover, Lewis, Garcia, Timmons, 2017)

Reflection

What decisions have you made recently that helped you rediscover your preferences or identity?

How did it feel the first time you had to make a decision without considering someone else's opinion?

How does 2 Timothy 1:7 encourage you as you make decisions on your own?

How are you feeling today?

S ☐

M ☐

T ☐

W ☐

T ☐

F ☐

S ☐

Weekly Prayer

Lord, Thank You for guiding me as I learn about myself again. Remind me that I am not alone—You walk beside me in every decision. Give me courage to choose boldly and live authentically. Amen.

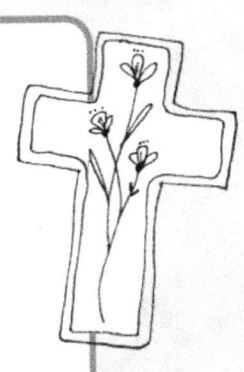

Letting Go and Holding On

At first glance, letting go and holding on seem like opposites, but when you're stepping into a new reality, you realize they *can* coexist. Moving forward often requires letting go of the past while clinging tightly to what matters most. The ability to do both at once can feel like chaos; it's also where healing begins.

For 32 years, I clung to a marriage, a family, and the life we had created. Letting go meant letting go of the dream of growing old together, the vision of a retirement beach house, and the family portraits I imagined with generations gathered in one frame. Divorce meant letting go of the belief that the good times could somehow outweigh the pain. I finally realized that many rights don't make up for repeated wrongs.

I was also letting go of the present because everything in my life immediately changed: where I lived, what I ate, and even how I moved through the day. Holiday traditions were replaced with new ones, but I assured my boys that the decisions we made that first Christmas were not decisions for every Christmas after; they were just decisions for now.

Routines changed and relationships were immediately altered. In the season of deep change, I needed people who would show up and help me choose a bed comforter, take me to dinner, sit quietly while I cried or just let me talk. I needed a friend who would text with me in the middle of the night when the dark felt heavy.

While letting go of the future, I was creating a void. It was just empty space and felt like uncertainty. But space is not empty when you trust God to fill it. Isaiah 41:10 assures us of God's promise of companionship and active involvement in our lives. Faith is knowing He already has plans for my future.

Letting go made room for peace, for clarity, and for healing.

Holding on to my faith, my people, and my worth gave me strength.

God never asked me to choose between letting go and holding on. He simply asked me to trust Him. In His hands, I can release what hurts and hold on to what heals.

Goodbye, Yesterday

Goodbye, yesterday
I'm livin' in the light of a new day
I won't waste another minute in my old ways
Praise the Lord, I've been born again

Goodbye, yesterday
The Spirit of the Lord is upon me
I've got resurrection in my veins
Praise the Lord, I've been born

Elevation Worship
(Furtick, Holiday, Wong, & Binion, 2024)

Reflection

What have you had to let go of—physically, emotionally, or spiritually—in this season of your life?

How have your relationships shifted since you began this journey?

How does Isaiah 41:10 bring you comfort or strength in moments of fear or doubt?

What are you grateful for this week?

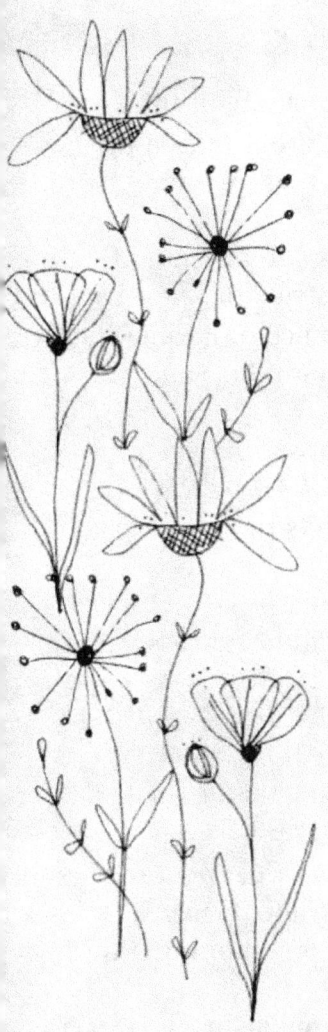

Weekly Prayer

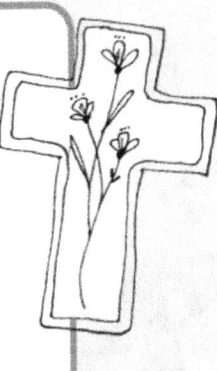

Lord, help me release what no longer serves my heart and hold tightly to what brings healing and hope. Give me courage to face the unknown, strength to walk forward, and faith to trust Your plan. Uphold me with Your love as I let go and begin again. Amen.

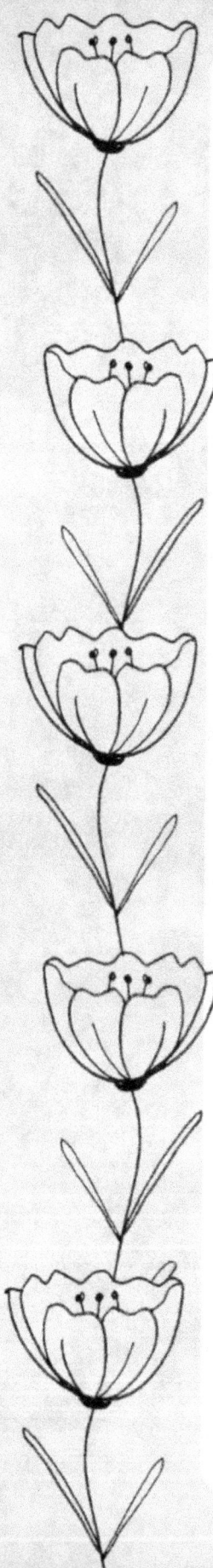

Asking for Help

Mountains of laundry. Mountains of work. Mountains of paperwork. Mountains can be overwhelming. When you first begin this journey, you feel like you are trudging uphill at a steep incline.

This journey has taught me more than I ever expected about the importance of asking for help. Thinking I had to figure it out on my own probably kept me in my marriage longer. But I was wrong.

When I started reaching out, calling friends, leaning on family, and sitting across from my therapist, I found a kind of strength I never knew before. I can't emphasize enough the importance of finding the right therapist. Take the time and find the right person for you.

One therapy session when we were discussing an upsetting event, she gave me a tool I now use regularly. It's called **GLAD** by David Altman, and it helps me ground myself when life feels too big.

> **G** – *Gratitude*: *What am I thankful for today?* Make a list! Not one or two things, but a long list. Nothing is too small to express gratitude for.
> **L** – *Learning*: *What did I learn about myself or the world?* I *am* strong. I can set up automatic payments for bills. I *can* find the right place on the computer to watch an international soccer game.
> **A** – *Accomplishment*: *What small (or big) thing did I get done?* I hosted dinner for my nieces and nephews at my new place. I found a cute picture frame for my mantel. I put together an end table.
> **D** – *Delight*: *What made me smile today?* This is my favorite because my therapist said I should "delight in the Lord and find the joy" in the situation. Looking for the bright side helps set a tone for self-talk.

When I pair GLAD with verses like Psalm 121, I feel a shift in my spirit. I'm reminded that seeking help isn't selfish or needy, it's necessary.

Asking for help isn't a sign of weakness, it means I trust that God works through the people He's placed around me. Mountains can be conquered.

> *"I lift up my eyes to the mountains—*
> *where does my help come from?*
> *My help comes from the Lord,*
> *the Maker of heaven and earth."*
>
> Psalm 121:1–2

He's working on me, still
Changing me piece by piece, still
Making me better, gonna do His thing
Don't care how long it takes 'til...

That I'm a sinner saved by grace
'Cause I need more every day
That's why
He's working on me, still

Crowder

(Crowder, Glover & Sojka, 2025)

Reflection

Psalm 121 begins with a question: *"Where does my help come from?"* How would you answer that question honestly right now?

Which part of the GLAD (Gratitude, Learning, Accomplishment, Delight) acronym feels most important for you today—and why?

What is one area in your life where you need help but haven't asked for it yet?

How are you feeling today?

S ☐

M ☐

T ☐

W ☐

T ☐

F ☐

S ☐

Weekly Prayer

Lord, Thank You for being my constant help and strength. When I feel overwhelmed, remind me to lift my eyes to You. Give me courage to ask for help – from You and from others. Amen.

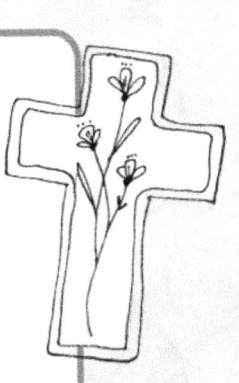

Reflections on Calm Water

Thinking back on my brother-in-law's comment about me being one of the strongest people he knew, I realized I didn't recognize myself anymore. I had lost myself in trying to be someone different, someone quiet, someone willing to hand over control. I'm not sure these were conscious decisions, but they were there. Then I heard the quote, "You can't see your reflection in boiling water."

This quote is most frequently used in relation to anger, but I think it's the perfect analogy for a divorce. When life is full of chaos, confusion, and pain, it's like trying to see your reflection in boiling water. Nothing is clear. You can't make sense of what's happening around you or inside you. You're just trying to survive the steam. Sometimes you pull back from the tension and become someone you never intended.

Jeremiah 33:6 signifies God's intention to restore, heal, and provide abundantly for His people, both physically and spiritually.

It's a beautiful assurance, but sometimes, it seems far away. During the hardest seasons of my life, I couldn't see the full extent of the pain I was in. I couldn't tell where the hurt began or what healing would look like. When I finally stepped out of the storm, when the secrets stopped simmering and the stress began to settle, the water got still. And in that stillness, I could finally see. Sadly, the reflection was not what I wanted to see.

I saw the truth. I saw who I had become, and in a lot of ways I didn't recognize myself. I was quick to anger over small things. I avoided hard conversations, and I lied to myself and my friends about my life. I could make sure everyone in the room was comfortable because taking care of others was easier than facing myself.

Choosing to leave was a strong act of self-love. I wanted to truly see myself in calm water.

Sometimes clarity only comes when we step away from the heat. When the water calms, our reflection becomes visible again. And with it, we begin to see hope.

> *"I will heal and reveal the abundance of peace and truth."*
>
> Jeremiah 33:6

I Know A Name

I know a name that can silence the roaring waves
I know a name that can empty out a grave
I know a name, it's the only name that saves
And it's worthy of all praise
I call You, Jesus
I call You, I call You Healer

Elevation Worship
& Brandon Lake
(Sooter , Furtick, Bentley & Lake, 2025)

Reflection

What did "boiling water" look like in your life?

Why is it so hard to be strong for ourselves, especially when we're used to being strong for others?

What has become clearer to you now that the "water" has calmed in your life?

What are you grateful for this week?

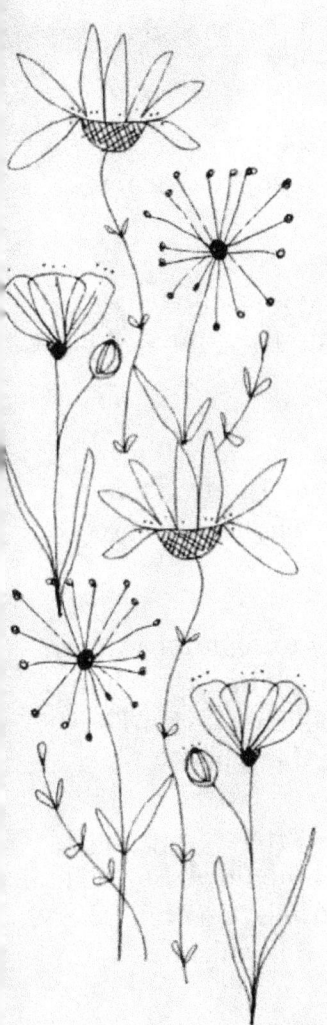

Weekly Prayer

Lord, when life feels like boiling water, calm my spirit and clear my vision. Help me step away from chaos and see myself through Your truth. Reveal what is broken and restore what is lost. In stillness, let me find You. Amen.

Clearing the FOG

Have you ever taught someone to drive? When you are teaching someone to drive your practice usually takes place during the day and in good weather. The better they get at that skill we can add obstacles like driving at night and driving in fog.

When you're in fog, you must reduce your speed, give lots of space between you and the car in front of you, and to use your low beams to highlight the road.

I heard something that resonated with me about divorce. The person was saying there are three reasons you can be manipulated to stay in a marriage: fear, obligation, or guilt. That's the FOG.

Fear – One of the biggest reasons anyone stays in a marriage that isn't working is fear. The fear of telling your children. The fear that people will learn the truth. The fear of being alone. The fear of the unknown.

Obligation - Don't I have an obligation to my family to fight for my marriage? Don't I have an obligation to the vows I took in a church in front of God to fight for my marriage? Is there an obligation that I have to this partner to try and "fix them" or "make them better" before walking away?

Guilt - I don't mean the correctly-placed guilt of the offender; I mean the guilt we place on ourselves when we think about ending our marriage. What example would I be to my children if I walked away? The guilt of losing a family is crippling.

We have to break out of the FOG of our decisions. I didn't deserve to stay in a marriage based on fear, obligation, and guilt. No one does.

Just like learning to drive in fog, if we reduce our speed (slow down and take a breath), make sure there is distance (creating space away), and use low beams to illuminate our path forward, we will soon be guided by the Light of the World to brighter days.

"We don't yet see things clearly. We're squinting in a fog, peering through a mist. But it won't be long before the weather clears, and the sun shines bright!"

1 Corinthians 13:12 (MSG)

Faithfully

It's been a long year, it almost took me down, I swear

But when my world broke into pieces
You were there faithfully
When I cried out to You, Jesus
You made a way for me

TobyMac

(Williams, McKeehan, Smith and Kuiper, 2024)

Reflection

Which part of the FOG—fear, obligation, or guilt—has been the hardest for you to recognize or release? Why?

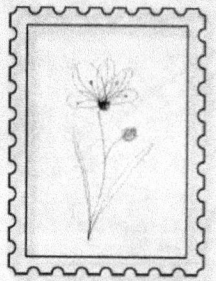

What does "walking in the light" look like for you today?

How can slowing down, creating space, and focusing on the path ahead help you break free from emotional or spiritual fog?

How are you feeling today?

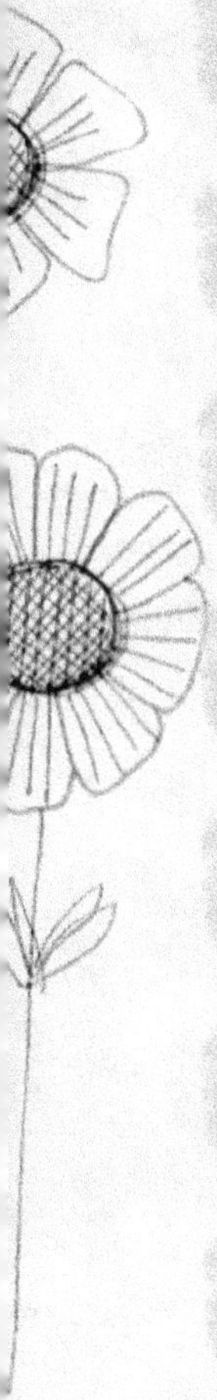

S ☐

M ☐

T ☐

W ☐

T ☐

F ☐

S ☐

Weekly Prayer

Lord, when life feels clouded by fear, obligation, and guilt, help me to slow down and seek Your light. Clear the fog from my heart and mind. Thank You for being my constant light. Amen.

Connecting My Heart and My Head

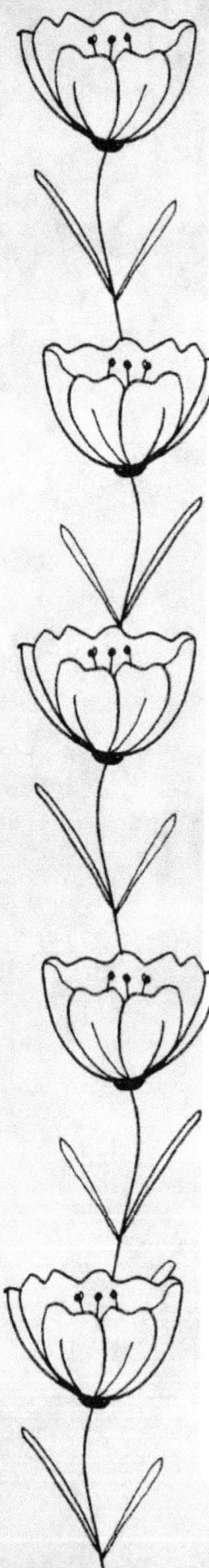

The Apostle Paul shows us in Romans 8:27 that we can align our heart and our head to move forward in wisdom and purpose. But, man, that's hard.

One of the most difficult hurdles I've faced is connecting my heart and my head. My heart was broken more than once by the actions of my ex. He was careless with it, and it will have scars forever.

During a late-night text conversation with a friend, I confessed that nights were the hardest. He gave me this advice.

"Nights can be tough, lonely. Brain in overdrive, always going into the darkest places. But that's where your strength will come from, coming through the other side of that darkness. Getting to the point where you understand it in your head AND your heart is when you can move on.

You will get to a point where you understand that it's not your fault. You will understand that it's not something you were lacking but something lacking in him. Then and only then, your brain will start asking excitedly..... What's next?"

These were such powerful and wise words from a dear friend.

When my heart was hurting, my head could hear those words of advice.

Romans 8:27 highlights that the "Spirit intercedes according to God's will," which suggests that when your heart and head are surrendered and aligned with God, you're empowered to move forward in the right direction.

Believe that God is working on your behalf, even when you feel conflicted.

Trust that God knows both your emotions and your thoughts. Move forward in alignment with God's will. He wants the best for your heart and your head.

> *"And he who searches our hearts knows the mind of the Spirit, because the Spirit intercedes for the saints according to the will of God."*
>
> Romans 8:27

Tell Your Heart to Beat Again

You're shattered like you've never been before
The life you knew in a thousand pieces on the floor
And words fall short in times like these
When this world drives you to your knees
You think you're never gonna get back
To the you that used to be

Danny Gokey
(Herms, Philips & West, 2014)

Reflection

When have you felt a disconnect between what your heart felt and what your head knew to be true?

Can you identify a moment where you started to view your story (even the painful parts) as part of your growth?

What would "moving forward in alignment with God's will" look like for you today?

What are you grateful for this week?

Weekly Prayer

Lord, you see my heart and know my thoughts. When they feel at odds, bring peace to the war within me. Thank you for the Spirit who intercedes when I cannot find the words. Help me trust Your will and walk forward with courage, clarity, and confidence in your plan. Amen.

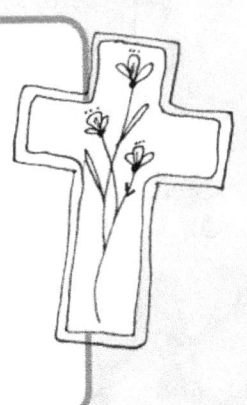

Keep Moving Forward

Divorce seems to bring your life to a standstill. Nothing feels the same; you don't know where to go or what to do. You don't feel married, but you don't feel single. You know what you didn't want in a marriage, but you aren't quite sure what you want in your life now. One of the best ways to learn about yourself is to keep moving.

When life feels overwhelming or uncertain, it can be hard to know where to begin. But God reminds us in Jeremiah 29:11 that He has a plan for our lives, and we can trust it's a good plan. "Plans to prosper you and not to harm you, plans to give you hope and a future." Wow! We want "hope and a future."

A friend who had been through divorce said, "When you can't sleep, do something. Don't just lie there staring at the clock, counting the hours until the alarm goes off. Get up and do anything that will clear your mind. Clean the kitchen. Sweep the floor. Do the laundry. Fill the emptiness with small accomplishments."

Even when I didn't have a reason to get up early, I made a point to set my alarm. I created a routine in my life even when I didn't want one. Believe it or not, when you keep moving, you are progressing. Each day you recover a bit more. Each day you become more of who you are meant to be.

But each day, you are progressing. It won't feel like it at first. It's a slow process and one you can't speed up. One day you look behind you and see just how far you've come. Who you were or what you accepted are forgotten and you are in a new place. So, don't stop.

Take one small step each day toward the life you want to build for tomorrow.

The promise in Jeremiah 29 doesn't require giant leaps; it invites faithful steps.

Each day, I had the opportunity to take one small action toward the life I was meant to live. I trusted that God was guiding my journey, even when the path felt slow. He guided my past, just as He guides my future. A hopeful future begins with today's decision to move forward.

"For I know the plans I have for you," declares the Lord, "plans to prosper you and not to harm you, plans to give you hope and a future."

Jeremiah 29:11

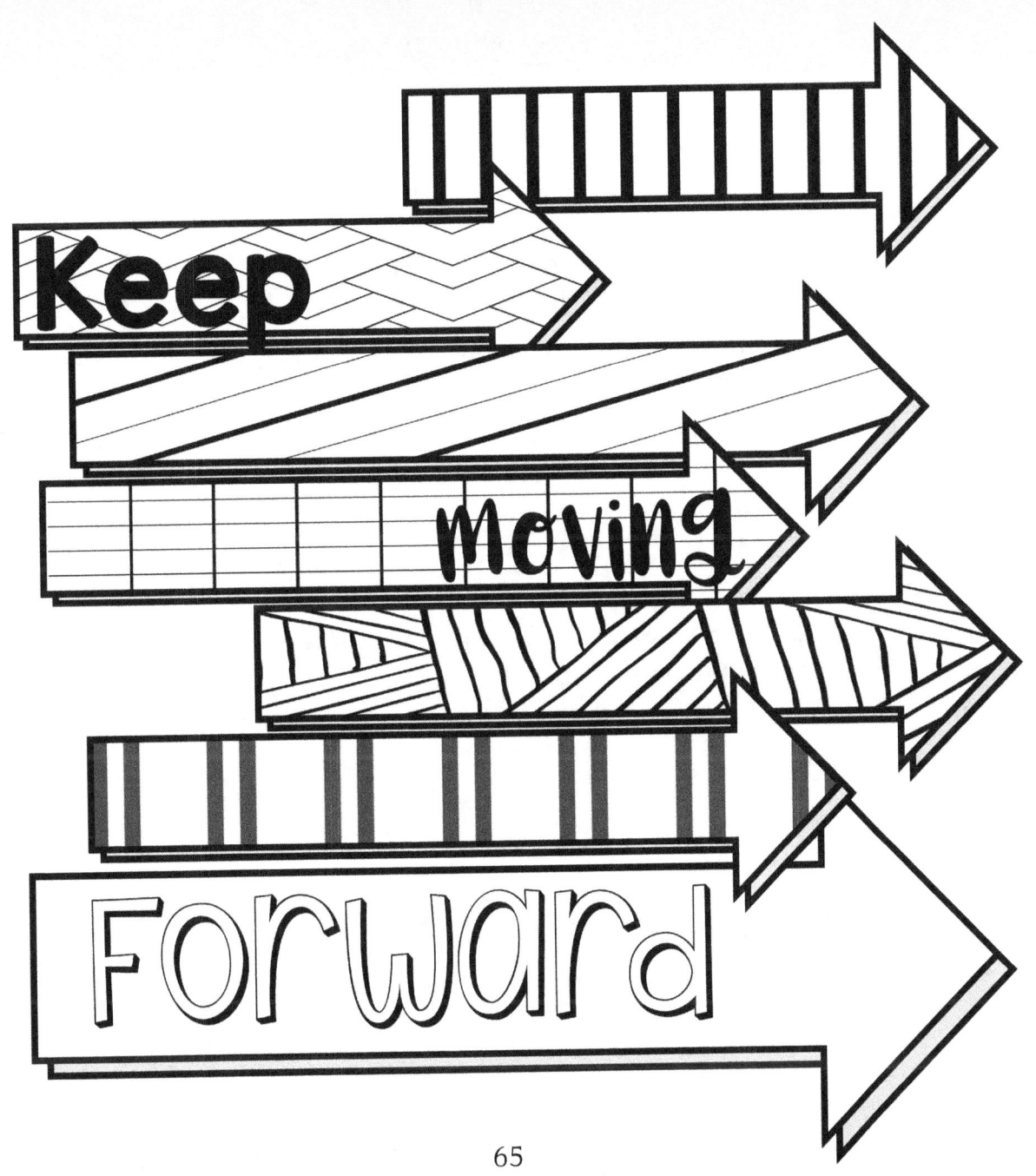

10,000 Reasons

The sun comes up, it's a new day dawning;
It's time to sing Your song again.
Whatever may pass and whatever lies before me,
Let me be singing when the evening comes.

Bless the Lord, O my soul,
Worship His holy Name.
Sing like never before, O my soul.
I'll worship Your holy Name.

Matt Redman
(Redman & Myrin, 2011)

Reflection

What does "keep moving" mean to you during seasons of waiting or healing?

What is one area of your life you need to surrender because it's out of your control?

What "faithful step" could you take today toward the life you want to build?

How are you feeling today?

S ☐

M ☐

T ☐

W ☐

T ☐

F ☐

S ☐

Weekly Prayer

Lord, when I feel stuck or weary, remind me that every small step matters. Help me trust Your plan even when I can't see the outcome. Give me strength to move forward with faith, courage, and hope, knowing that You guide my steps toward healing, purpose, and a future filled with promise. Amen.

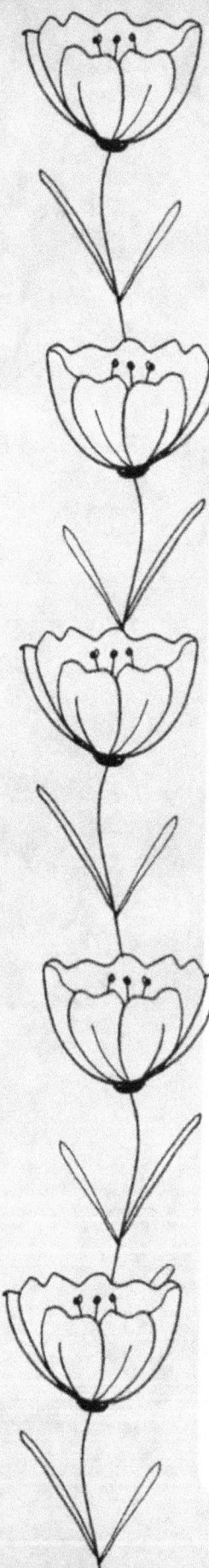

Nourishing Your Body

When I first heard someone say, *"You can't heal if you don't nourish your body,"* I honestly brushed it off. I was functioning. I was surviving. That had to be enough, right?

Over time, I began to realize that nourishment is about more than food, it's about caring for the body God gave me. Nourishment includes food, rest, and movement. And in grief or transition, each of those can get thrown off balance.

Some people eat when they're sad. Some people can't eat at all. I'm one of the ones who eats. The problem is I don't eat well. True confession: I've eaten ice cream for dinner more than once. And you know what? That's okay. As long as it doesn't become a pattern that robs me of health or strength, I can give myself a scoop of grace. Creating a plan for food matters. Nothing is worse than being hungry and not having something nourishing within reach.

Intentional nourishment also means moving my body, even when I don't feel like it. I had unintentionally taken a break from Jazzercise™ when I first made my decision to leave my marriage. I just couldn't convince myself to get up and go. Then one day, I realized I missed the ladies, and that motivated me. I knew even if I could only give half effort, they would welcome me. I was able to confide in these ladies and that community of women showed up for me in ways I didn't expect every single time.

Rest can be tricky, too. Sometimes sleep comes easily. Sometimes it doesn't. At first, on days when I talked to the lawyer, I knew I'd be restless that night. The fear of "getting it wrong" is louder in the dark.

I've learned that true rest isn't laziness. True rest is considered obedience to the God who created Sabbath. Sometimes rest means a midday nap. Sometimes it's winding down with herbal tea.

Healing requires energy and energy requires care.

So today, whether it's a healthy breakfast, a good sweat, or a peaceful nap, do it for the glory of God.

> *"So, whether you eat or drink, or whatever you do, do all to the glory of God."*
>
> 1 Corinthians 10:31

I keep fighting voices in my mind
that say I'm not enough
Every single lie that tells me I will never measure up

You say I am strong when I think I am weak...
You say I am held when I am falling short...

Lauren Daigle
(Daigle and Ingram, 2018)

Reflection

Which part of your self-care—food, movement, or rest—feels the most out of balance right now? What is one step towards fixing it?

What kind of movement or physical activity brings you joy or peace? How can you make space for that in your current season?

How does remembering that your body is a gift from God change the way you think about caring for it?

What are you grateful for this week?

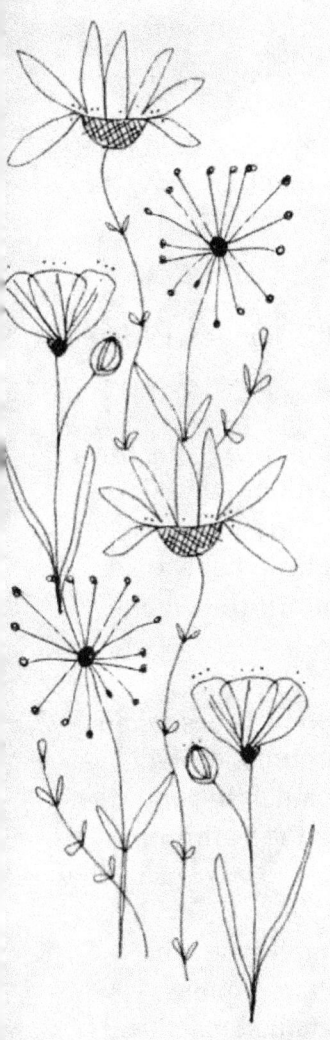

Weekly Prayer

Lord, Thank You for the body You gave me. Help me honor it with nourishment, movement, and rest. On days when I feel weak, remind me that You are my strength. Teach me to care for myself with grace, knowing that healing is holy work. Amen.

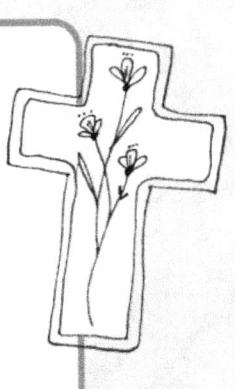

Hope in the Future

When you're walking through divorce, hope can feel like a foreign language. It's hard to picture a future that looks anything like peace, joy, or even stability. Everything familiar has been stripped away or rewritten. The future seems blurry at best and terrifying at worst.

At one time, I could only imagine what the rest of my life would look like with my ex in it. Vacations, holidays, and retirement are now all incomplete puzzles with pieces missing. And yet, Hebrews 11:1 reminds me that faith begins where sight ends.

Hope isn't about having a perfectly detailed plan; it's about trusting that God still has a plan, even when ours has fallen apart.

We don't always see God's plan laid out in front of us like plans for a new home. God reveals His plan to us slowly and deliberately. God speaks to us about being a "lamp unto my feet." He doesn't speak about being a spotlight. You see, a lamp provides a little light to see a little further on our path. We aren't given a spotlight to the whole path.

This makes me think of camping as a child. There were times when we had to walk across the campground to the bathrooms at night, with a flashlight lighting our path. We couldn't see much beyond the steps in front of us, but we just kept going knowing the bathroom was at the end of the path.

God's lamp is just that, guidance to continue moving. Those who have faith also have hope and believe that the path is uniquely designed for our benefit. We only have to see the small steps ahead to follow in His love.

Remembering that the sun comes after every dark night can give us peace. God directs us to the Son, who is the Light in all circumstances.

Just as Hebrews 11 reminds us, hope has faith in tomorrow. Hope has belief in a better day. Hope is knowing God has a plan for me and knowing His path will take me where I will thrive.

"Now Faith is confidence in what we hope for and assurance about what we do not see."

Hebrews 11:1

I'm tryna keep my hopes up, keep my head up
Keep my eyes up, some things are easier said than done
Every dark night gonna see the sun
Sooner or later
I guess I'm waiting for some better days
Some better days

Ryan Ellis

(Ellis, Nauriyal, and Wong, 2024)

Reflection

When has hope felt out of reach during your divorce journey, and what helped you find it again?

Ryan Ellis sings, "Every dark night gonna see the sun, sooner or later." What is a "dark night" you walked through to see the sun?

Can you name one thing, no matter how small, that gives you hope for the future?

How are you feeling today?

S ☐

M ☐

T ☐

W ☐

T ☐

F ☐

S ☐

Weekly Prayer

Heavenly Father, When the future feels uncertain, help me hold tightly to hope. Remind me that You see the road ahead, even when I cannot. Strengthen my faith, steady my heart, and guide my steps. Let me trust that better days are coming—because You are already there. Amen.

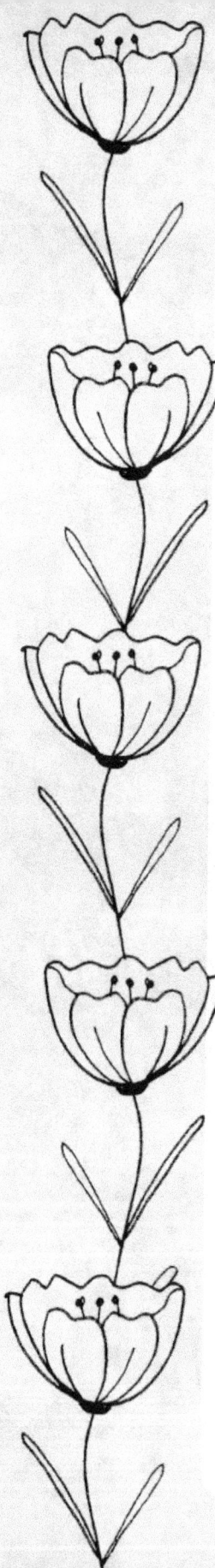

Don't Get Stuck in the Wallow

Wallowing is normal. It's hard to be upbeat and positive all the time. Every now and then, the weight of those hard decisions catches you off guard.

For me, it happened one weekend in my new condo. I had organized, unpacked, and arranged everything for weeks. And then I found a picture of vacation at the beach. Family fun and smiles for days.

I spent that weekend feeling sorry for myself. I didn't reach out to the people who said they'd be there. I just wallowed. I played the *"Why me?"* game and spent hours on the couch and in bed crying.

It's okay to wallow. Life is changing, and we're making a million decisions we never wanted to face. Sometimes it feels like life is happening to us, even when we are the ones who initiate the change. We just can't get stuck.

Sometimes we look for help when the answer is already in us. Isaiah 43:2 reminds us that no matter how deep the muck gets, He is there with us. We must know that after a valley, there is a peak and after rain, there is sunshine because God's promise delivers. Every time.

The Monday after my wallowing weekend, I decided to put on my big girl pants and get motivated. I loved my outfit, my hair looked good, and I took a picture and sent it to my sister with a text:

He won't win. I will be fine.

Now, I do reach out to when the wallow creeps in. My best friend knows if she gets a call from me in the evening, I'm problem laying awake in bed upset. She always answers. One night, I texted another friend:

Today was hard.

For the next hour we texted trips we should take and food we should eat.

Let's go to Italy for pasta. Let's do Alaska for crab legs.
Let's go to Maine for the lobster.

Such a fun way to get out of a funk. Lean on your people and lean on the Lord.

"When you pass through the waters, I will be with you; and when you pass through the rivers, they will not sweep over you. When you walk through the fire, you will not be burned; the flames will not set you ablaze."

Isaiah 43:2

Then Christ Came

I was searching for a reason
To believe that I could ever really matter
I was hoping, I was reaching
So desperate for my soul to find its Savior

Then Christ came
Changing everything
He took my sin and shame away

Mercy Me

(Ingram, Leonard, Wickham & Millard, 2021)

Reflection

What does "wallowing" look like for you?

How does Isaiah 43:2 speak to you in seasons when you feel stuck?

Write one you can do to get "unstuck" when you find yourself wallowing?

What are you grateful for this week?

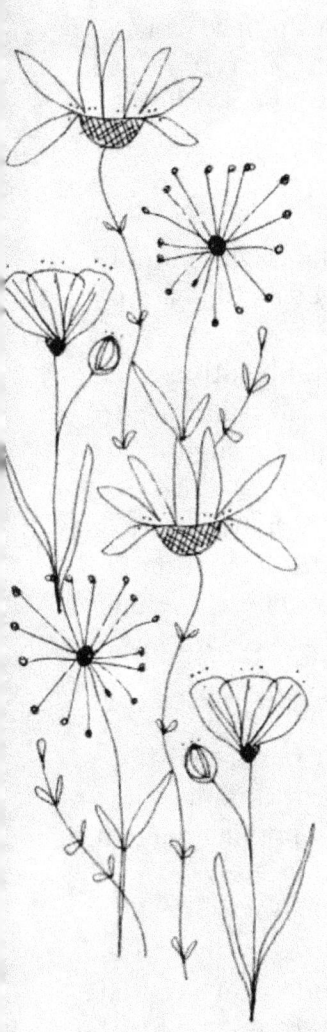

Weekly Prayer

Lord, When I find myself stuck in sadness or self-pity, remind me that You are with me in the mess. Help me feel Your presence and strength, even in the stillness. Lift me out of the muck and set my feet on solid ground.
Amen.

Feeling All the Feels

When you talk about feelings during this process, sometimes it feels like you are carved open for all to see AND your emotions are running wild. One minute you are feeling sad, then the next you're content, and then, almost immediately, you're feeling sorry for yourself. Each event, each day, and each moment can be a roller coaster of emotions.

It's normal. Learning to live a new life involves "all the feels." To me, it seems as if the expression, "learning to fly the plane while building it" was directly referring to learning to live while getting divorced.

John Deloney, a popular radio personality and mental health expert says that divorce is "deeply painful and traumatic." He continues to say that you "can't skip the emotions, you have to go through it."

One session my therapist asked me this question , "What is your first emotion when you think about this divorce?" Without hesitation I said, "relief." Then I let out a huge breath. I was so many emotions, but mostl I was relieved. His betrayals forced me to live with my guard up, always waiting for "the next time."

"Feeling sad after making the right decision doesn't mean that it wasn't the right decision." This isn't attributed to any author, but they certainly hit the nail on the head. I am sad my marriage ended. I worked hard on it but ending it was the right decision.

I'm also angry it ended. I'm angry he didn't want it as badly as I did. I'm angry he treated my love so callously and he took it for granted. I'm angry we have to cheer on our children separately, maybe for the moment, maybe forever.

I'm happy I stood up for myself and I'm happy I put myself first. I'm happy my children are supportive of me. I am also happy to set an example of healing after trauma.

Philippians 4:6-7 helps us know that whatever we bring to God, He will help protect our "hearts and minds." All we have to do is ask. The scripture says "by prayer and petition, with thanksgiving" come to Him for strength. Besides, that plane you're building will likely take you on great adventures.

"Do not be anxious about anything, but in every situation, by prayer and petition, with thanksgiving, present your requests to God. And the peace of God, which transcends all understanding, will guard your hearts and your minds in Christ Jesus."

Philippians 4:6-7

Praise You in the Storm

And I'll praise You in this storm
And I will lift my hands
For You are who You are, No matter where I am

And every tear I've cried
You hold in Your hand
You never left my side, And though my heart is torn
I will praise You in this storm

Natalie Grant
(Herms & Hall, 2005)

Reflection

What is your gut reaction when you think of your primary emotion during this time?

Which emotion do you struggle the most to express or allow yourself to feel—and why do you think that is?

How can you practice bringing your emotions to God in prayer and thanksgiving, as Philippians 4:6-7 encourages?

How are you feeling today?

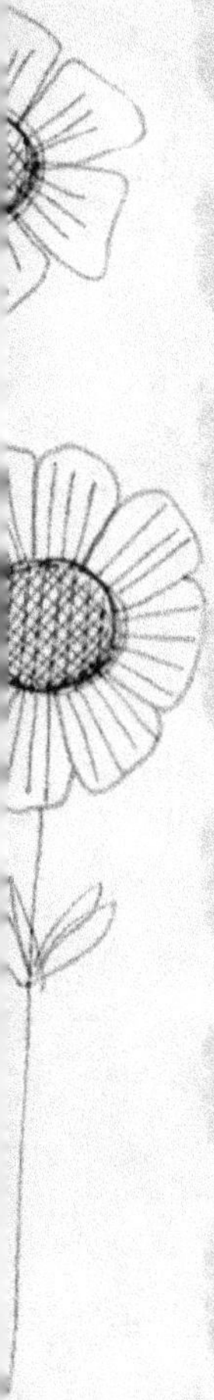

S ☐

M ☐

T ☐

W ☐

T ☐

F ☐

S ☐

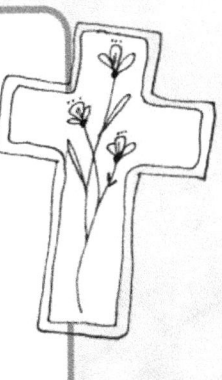

Weekly Prayer

Lord, thank you for creating me with the capacity to feel deeply. Help me not to fear my emotions but to bring each one to You with honesty and trust. Guard my heart and mind with Your peace and remind me that healing comes through feeling. In Jesus' name, Amen.

Curating My Circle

When you're walking through a season like divorce, your circle matters more than ever. The ones who show up, check in, sit with you in the mess, and remind you who you are when you forget are your people. These people are the embodiment of Proverbs 17:17. They love at all times, not just the convenient or easy ones. They're not scared off by your grief, your anger, or your silence. They are the ones born for adversity, your sisters and brothers in the storm.

Your circle should involve people who cheer you on but who also let you exhale. People who allow you to sit in a space and talk and people who let you just sit quietly without talking. People who make you take a shower and take you to dinner. People who ask you to go to a hole-in-the-wall place to watch a guitar player on a Wednesday night just because you needed to get out. You need these people.

I've also had to realize not everyone can walk this path with me. Some people I thought would be there, simply weren't. And that hurts, but I've come to understand it without judgment. Everyone is carrying something. Sometimes your pain reminds them of their own.

During the separation, I was disorganized and felt like I wasn't a good friend. I missed birthdays. I forgot anniversaries. I didn't reach out often enough, and I couldn't seem to remember things a true friend should. A friend told me about the pendulum of friendship. Sometimes one friend can't give the same at the same time. One friend must take the lead and handle the invitations and check ins. The feelings, the love and the intentions are the same, but you aren't the same during this life change.

Some of the people in my friendship circle I've known my whole life while some I've met more recently. Some of my circle are people I went to college with, worked with, or who had children on my children's soccer teams. Some friends are divorced. Most are not.

One day I received a text.

I have always believed that you should surround yourself with people who will fight for you in rooms you aren't in. Know that you have done that.

It took my breath away. People who are in rooms I'm not in are fighting for me! I've also heard, "God helps remove people from your life because He heard conversations you haven't." Divorce is a time when true friendship thrives. Proverbs 17 reminds us we need friends who love at all times, not just the easy ones.

> *"A friend loves at all times,
> and a brother is born of adversity."*
>
> Proverbs 17:17

85

Good God Almighty

You say Your love goes on forever,
that Your mercy never stops
So why would I assume
You'd be somebody that You're not
Like sun in the morning,
I know You're gonna be there every day
So what on earth could make me be afraid?

Good God almighty
I hope You'll find me

Crowder

(Crowder, Glover & Sojka, 2021)

Reflection

Who are the people in your life right now that make you feel seen, safe, and supported?

Have you experienced the quiet grief of a friendship that faded during your divorce? How do you feel about it?

Think about someone who surprised you by showing up during your hardest moments. What made their support feel meaningful?

What are you grateful for this week?

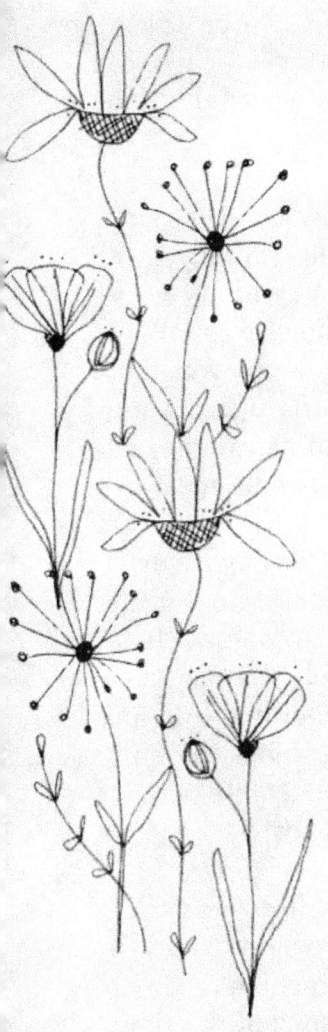

Weekly Prayer

Lord, thank you for the gift of true friendship—those who walk with us through sorrow and joy. Help me to cherish those who lift me up and release those who cannot stay. Guide me in curating a circle of love, truth, and peace. Surround me with grace-filled, faithful hearts. Amen.

Discovering Solitude

There's a difference between being alone and choosing solitude. For so long, the idea of being alone felt like punishment to me, like something was missing or someone had left. I did, however, enjoy the occasional couple of days that my husband would travel for work. I could spend that time doing what I wanted. Since it was only for a limited time, I wasn't lonely.

In a matter of a few months, I was in a condo by myself every single day. It was the first time I'd ever lived alone. I went from my childhood home to my college dorm to an apartment with a roommate to getting married. I always had someone else to talk to about nothing or watch television with at night. Someone was there to check my outfit or give me an opinion about dinner plans. There was a comfort in having someone else there. I've come to realize, I'd rather be alone than with someone who didn't appreciate me.

Don't get me wrong, sometimes I am lonely. Day after day of just being by myself can be lonely, but if that's the trade, I'd do it again. One of the first weekends in my new place, I decided to go with a friend for an overnight stay in a town close by. It felt strange that I could just go without telling anyone. I called my sister and told her what I was doing. She laughed that I was reporting to her, but she understood. Since that time, I've become more comfortable with living alone and I don't tell my sister every time I leave.

Solitude can feel like a cozy chair and a great book. It doesn't take much to get comfortable. I did discover that my favorite tv show of all time was on my tv 24/7/365. If I need noise or people talking, I turn on the tv. I know it seems silly, but the familiarity of the show and the characters is comforting.

In this season of rebuilding, I've come to realize that solitude isn't about emptiness. It's about stepping away from the noise to reconnect with myself, with peace, and with living a life God has ordained. God only wants the best for me and if being alone is the best for now, I'll wait on the rest.

Deuteronomy 31 assures me that God will not forsake me or abandon me and that's good enough for me.

> *"The Lord himself goes before you and will be with you; He will not leave you nor forsake you. Do not be discouraged."*
>
> Deuteronomy 31:8

Another in the Fire

There was another in the fire, Standing next to me
There was another in the waters, Holding back the seas
And should I ever need reminding
Of how I've been set free

There is a cross that bears the burden
Where another died for me
There is another in the fire

Hillsong UNITED
(Davenport & Houston, 2019)

Reflection

What is the difference between loneliness and solitude in your own life?

How does the verse from Deuteronomy 31:8 speak to your comfort—or discomfort—with being alone?

Can you recall a moment when you truly heard your own voice in the quiet?

How are you feeling today?

S ☐

M ☐

T ☐

W ☐

T ☐

F ☐

S ☐

Weekly Prayer

Lord, thank you for meeting me in the quiet. In the stillness of solitude, help me feel Your presence more deeply. Remind me I am never truly alone—You go before me and stay beside me. Let peace replace fear, and may I find comfort in Your nearness. Amen.

Reclaiming My Faith

When the boys started playing soccer, there weren't enough fields in the area to have all the games on Saturdays. So, we played soccer on Sundays. That's why we stopped going to church initially.

We went for the *big* days (Christmas and Easter) and depending on soccer tournaments we went on Father's Day and Mother's Day. However, I can remember one Mother's Day on the soccer field in the middle of a hurricane getting soaking wet and being given a very wilted single stem flower as a gift. All I could do was laugh! I also convinced myself that we didn't need to go to church since we were with our family. The church was put on the shelf.

Several months into my separation, my sister and her family were singing in a local church. She said they had committed to singing on a regular basis. I'm not sure why, but I asked her to take me with her the next time she went. Instead, my sister said, "Go with us this week. We're going to a new church, and you should go with us." I said yes, and I loved it.

It was so different from the church I grew up in. It was a contemporary service with a live praise band and the contemporary Christian music that I was listening to on the radio. I also got to go with my sister. She has become my best friend and spending time with her has been a saving grace. I also liked being anonymous for a while. No one knew me, so no one knew I was going through a divorce. I wasn't greeted with looks of pity.

I looked forward to going to church. I wanted to sing, worship, and be surrounded by people of faith. It didn't hurt that the first sermon was called, "What is Real Love?" I swear, I couldn't make this up. Who else but God? I felt like He was talking directly to me to confirm I needed church.

In Psalm 51, King David asked to be taken back to the "joy of your salvation" after he had sinned. He needed joy and salvation. Like David, I needed those, too. I had been raised in the church, but the church had been pushed aside. Now it was time to go back. Even though I had pushed the church away, God never gave up on me.

Sundays are joyful again and my faith is growing every day.

> *"Restore to me the joy of your salvation, and uphold me with a willing spirit, to sustain me."*
>
> Psalm 51:12

Church (Take Me Back)

Oh, take me back
To the place that feels like home
To the people I can depend on
To the faith that's in my bones
Take me back
To a preacher and a verse
Where they've seen me at my worst
To the love I had at first
Oh, I want to go to church.

Cochran & Co.
(Cochran, Fowler & Kuiper, 2021)

Reflection

Have there been seasons in your life when faith took a backseat?

How can community, family, church, or friends, support you in reclaiming your faith?

What role does worship (music, prayer, scripture) play in reconnecting with God?

What are you grateful for this week?

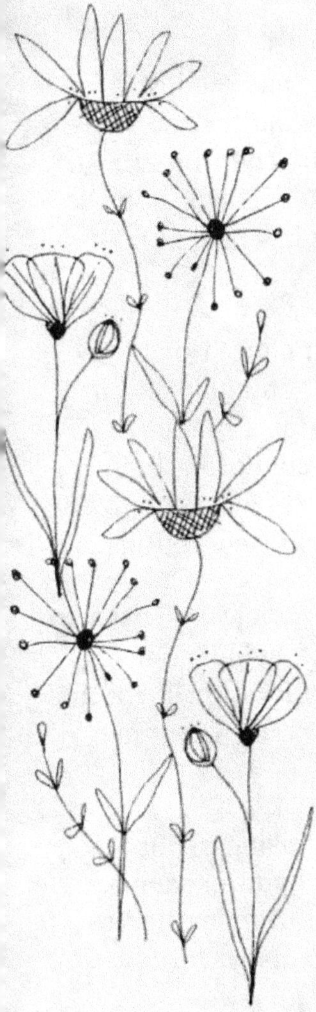

Weekly Prayer

Lord, restore the joy I once knew in Your presence. Renew my spirit with hope, peace, and purpose. Thank You for drawing me back with grace and love. Help me walk forward in faith, surrounded by community and anchored in You. I want to come home to You. Amen.

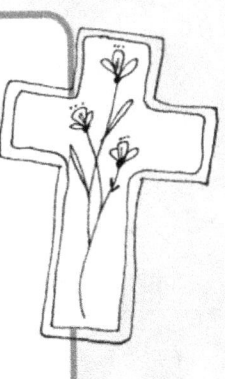

Building New Habits

Starting a new life means building new habits. After divorce, everything felt unfamiliar, even the small things. I wasn't just rebuilding a routine; I was rebuilding *a life*.

So, I started small. I found a journal for women that had a daily devotional and coloring page. I bought new markers and became intentional about my faith and reading His word. The coloring was so calming and meditative. I also spent time listening to His word on the radio through contemporary Christian music. Music has helped me heal and grow.

As funny as it sounds, I started making my bed each day. Prior to my divorce, we were in the habit of pulling up the sheet and blanket but not entirely making the bed. Now, I do. Each day, as part of my morning routine, I make the bed complete with the comforter, the pillows with shams and, yes, the accent pillows too. It feels good to come upstairs and see a freshly made bed. Small task. New routine.

Because my downstairs is an open floor plan, I hate to leave dishes in the sink or mess on the counter. I will have to admit, living alone doesn't require very many dishes. I use a dish and a fork for lunch. I wash it and put in the drying rack in the sink. Then, I use the same dish and fork for dinner. It's a perk of living alone.

I have always been good at making decisions in my business, but obviously not in my personal life. I had fallen into a habit of saying, "It doesn't matter to me" or "Whatever you want." I have learned to voice my opinions and help make decisions with friends. I will put my ideas out there. I had to build that new habit.

I am also intentional about telling people in my lives that I love them. I want people to know they are important to me. And, as you know, I created a new habit by attending church. I went whenever I was in town, even if it meant I went alone.

Psalm 40:2 reminds me that God didn't just pull me out of an unhealthy relationship; He planted me on something solid. Each step forward is a new habit, and each habit is a declaration that I'm not who I used to be. I'm growing into who God is calling me to be. As I build new habits, I'm also building a new life firmly rooted in grace.

> *"He lifted me out of the slimy pit, out of the mud and mire; He set my feet upon a rock and made my footsteps firm."*
>
> Psalm 40:2

Good Plans

He has good plans
He has good plans for me
So, I will take heart in deserts and gardens
He has good plans
He has good plans for me
If I know my Father
I know my Father has good plans

Red Rocks Worship
(Espy & Miller, 2023)

Reflection

Can you name a new habit that's helping you feel more grounded or peaceful today?

Why do you think old routines—even unhealthy ones—can be hard to release?

What would it look like to invite God into your daily habits, one small step at a time?

How are you feeling today?

S ☐

M ☐

T ☐

W ☐

T ☐

F ☐

S ☐

Weekly Prayer

Lord, Thank You for lifting me up and setting my feet on solid ground. Help me build new habits that reflect Your peace, strength, and purpose. Guide my steps each day as I learn to walk in healing, hope, and the joy of new beginnings. Amen.

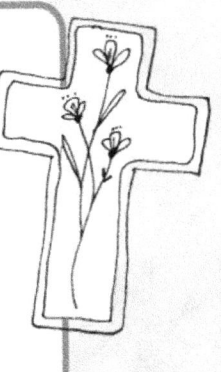

Grief Will Come

There's no denying the sadness of the divorce process. Even when you have a moment of complete clarity and you know in the depths of your soul that divorce is the only choice, it's still sad.

Grief is inevitable because you have lost what you knew and what you thought would be forever. I have experienced all the stages of grief (denial, anger, bargaining, depression, and acceptance). Grief isn't a straight line. It isn't a checklist. It isn't the same for everyone. Some stages will reoccur. You think you're doing well and all of a sudden, you'll be mad all over again or at the drop of a hat, you'll start crying about what was destroyed. Grief of a failed marriage is expected. I also believe I started grieving my marriage long before I left.

Another grief that is expected is the loss of the ex-spouse's family. You are no longer "in" the family. I was taken out of the family group text, and while it made sense, it hurt. I loved them as part of me for more than 30 years and I love them now. I had nothing against them, but they were collateral damage, and I understood that was a two-way street.

Unfortunately, there is an unexpected grief with your divorce; it's the grief with losing other people in your life. There will be friends who can't be there for you, and it hurts. You know their background or their trauma, and you realize your divorce can be triggering for them. They may be protecting themselves. Sometimes, you don't see it coming. Sometimes, it feels like another rejection in a terrible process. And there is grief.

The one thing to remember is that regardless of the grief, God is there always. Isaiah 66 tells you that he will protect you and comfort you, like a mother. His love and support will be constant.

Grief is the body's way of processing an event so monumental it changes us. Divorce is one of those events. Allowing the body time to grieve is the only way to truly heal. We won't be the same person, but I believe we become a better version of ourselves.

Fortunately, for us, God is the ultimate healer. He can take the broken and make it whole again.

> *"As a mother comforts her child, so will I comfort you; and you will be comforted over Jerusalem."*
>
> Isaiah 66:13

Battle Belongs

When all I see is the battle
You see my victory
When all I see is the mountain
You see a mountain moved
And as I walk through the shadow
Your love surrounds me
There's nothing to fear now
For I am safe with You

Phil Wickham
(Wickham, 2021)

Reflection

Which stage of grief has been most difficult for you to navigate during or after divorce, and why?

In what ways can you give yourself grace as you experience grief that doesn't follow a straight line or clear timeline?

How does the reminder that *"the battle belongs to God"* change how you approach your grief and healing?

What are you grateful for this week?

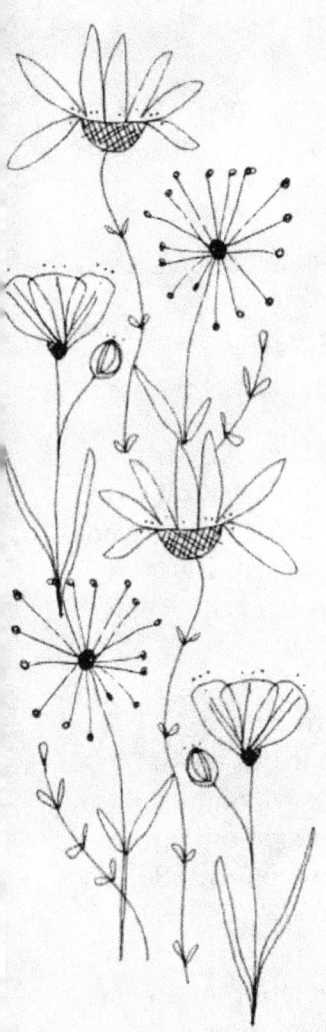

Weekly Prayer

Lord, Thank You for walking with me through the grief I didn't expect. Comfort my heart as only You can. Help me release the pain, the people, and the plans I've lost. Remind me daily that Your love surrounds me and that healing is possible in Your presence. Amen.

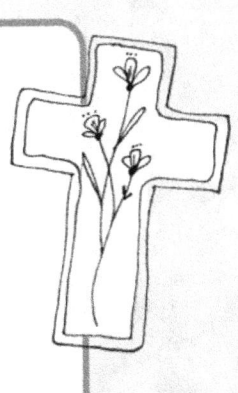

Power in Gentleness

You may be surprised that I'm talking about gentleness in the middle of divorce but stick with me. Gentleness isn't weakness; it's power that is under control. That's what true strength looks like.

Gentleness can be in the way we handle ourselves and how we speak to ourselves. Gentleness can be in the way we speak about our soon-to-be ex or how we speak about him to our children.

When I decided that I would be getting divorced, I delivered it clearly to my ex. Except for a few angry moments, I refused to scream. I refused to argue. I refused to debate. I said my peace, and I was done.

I also handled my words to my children with gentleness. I didn't provide intimate details about his indiscretions. I didn't ask them to be mad at their dad. I didn't ask them to be on my side. There is no side in a divorce for children, except if safety is a concern. I just wanted my children to know I understood my choice and the ripple effect it had on our family.

I have also learned to be gentle in the way I speak to myself. I thought I was being strong when I was silent. It's hard to look at a picture in a rearview mirror and not judge it. That's why hindsight is so perfect. Hindsight is judging our past with what we know in the future. I am giving myself grace for becoming a "new me" at 58. She is learning to love herself, even with her past.

A posture of gentleness can speak volumes over a position of power, but it isn't any less powerful. God doesn't call us to gentleness because He wants us to be passive. He calls us to it because He knows it reflects His character.

When we choose gentleness, we aren't stepping back in the shadows; we're stepping into grace. And that grace has power to change us and those around us. When Paul writes, "Let your gentleness be evident to all. The Lord is near," he reminds us that our posture matters—especially when life feels heavy. He isn't saying to be quiet or invisible; he's saying to live in a way that shows restraint, kindness, and clarity, even when it would be easier to explode or withdraw.

> *"Let your gentleness be evident to all.*
> *The Lord is near."*

Philippians 4:5

Gentle Like Jesus

Teach me how to be
Just like Christ my King
Help me be gentle like Jesus
For He was humble
Spirit come soften my heart
Help me be
Gentle like Jesus

Sovereign Grace Music
(Sczebel & Twining, 2009)

Reflection

How does your definition of gentleness shift when you think of it as "power under control"?

In what areas of your life—past or present—have you chosen gentleness when anger or bitterness felt easier?

How does Philippians 4:5 speak to your current season of life or healing?

How are you feeling today?

S ☐

M ☐

T ☐

W ☐

T ☐

F ☐

S ☐

Weekly Prayer

Lord, teach me the strength found in gentleness. Help me speak with grace, act with calm, and reflect Your love even in hard moments. Let gentleness guide my healing and become a quiet testimony of Your power within me. Amen.

Embracing My Independence

There's a unique kind of freedom that comes with regaining your independence, especially after years in a marriage where decisions were shared, identities blended, and boundaries often blurred. In my journey, that freedom hasn't just been about physical space or legal documents. It's been a deep, spiritual reclaiming of who I am and who God is calling me to be.

Regaining independence has meant breaking free of things that blocked my ability to live authentically, make choices, and chart my own path. It has meant setting new boundaries and rediscovering a strong sense of self. Along the way, I've learned to embrace self-reliance, recognizing that I am capable and equipped because God created me with gifts, wisdom, and discernment.

Sometimes, that discernment means you ask for help and sometimes it means you fix something yourself. When my HVAC was making my condo 77 degrees at night, I called a friend. (It wasn't "user error", by the way.) When I bought a table for my den that came in 100 pieces, I did it myself. Both felt good.

2 Corinthians 3:17 speaks of a freedom that isn't rooted in rebellion but in living a new life. Over this last year, I've been able to overcome fears and self-doubt. This new life isn't about indulging in whatever I want. It's about living a life how God intended, growing into a life of purpose and peace. More than anything, this freedom has led to changes in me.

That kind of freedom naturally leads to purposeful living. The more I trust His path, the more clearly I see the calling God has placed on my life. I'm not just existing; I'm stepping into meaning and mission.

No longer driven by the fear of judgment or the pressure to stay in my marriage, I can step out as my true self. I decide where my time and efforts are focused. I put my energy into living a life full of truth, not secrets. I'm also learning how to cultivate authentic relationships, rooted in truth and grace.

And through it all, I've come to understand the beauty of not just independence, but independence with God's help. I'm not doing this alone. I'm relying on friends, family and my faith.

"*Now the Lord is the Spirit, and where the Spirit of the Lord is, there is freedom.*"

2 Corinthians 3:17

There is Freedom

Hear the heavenly roar
Of every heart set free
Hear the chains of shame hit the ground
When the people of God sing

Where the Spirit of the Lord is, there is freedom
We'll be dancin' through the darkness
'cause we believe it

Josh Baldwin
(Fowler, Hulse & Baldwin, 2022)

Reflection

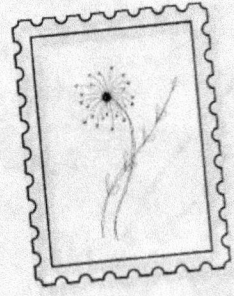

In what areas of your life have you begun to reclaim your identity and make independent choices?

How has the Holy Spirit helped you overcome internal struggles like fear, doubt, or insecurity?

How are you leaning on God, community, or Scripture as you build this new chapter of your life?

What are you grateful for this week?

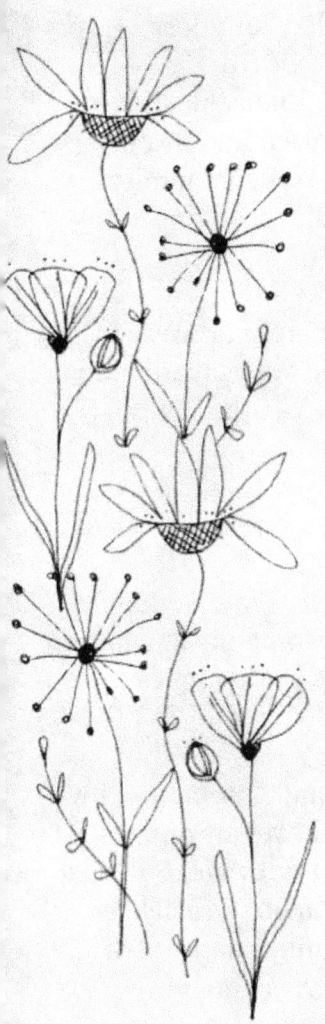

Weekly Prayer

Lord, Thank You for the freedom that comes through Your Spirit. Help me walk boldly in this new independence, trusting Your guidance. Renew my mind, reshape my heart, and lead me into the life You've prepared. Amen.

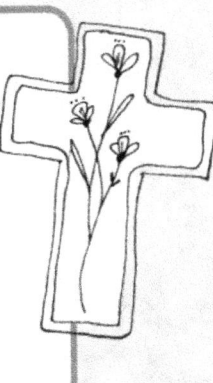

Reclaiming Confidence

Talking has never bothered me. I've spoken in classrooms, at School Board meetings, addressed the Virginia Department of Education as Vice Chair of the Governor's Teacher Cabinet, and led countless teacher workshops nationwide. As a member of the Board of Directors for the International Literacy Association, I had the surreal honor of interviewing Shaquille O'Neal in front of attendees at our St. Louis conference. Whether is is 30 5-year-olds, 100 community members, 200 educators or 8,000 conference attendees, talking doesn't scare me. (All my friends just said, "Amen.)

On the surface, my confidence was unshakable. Privately, however, everything crumbled when I discovered my husband was cheating on me. The betrayal was devastating, and I told no one. As the betrayals grew, my confidence waned.

I wore external confidence like a mask, hiding my real pain.

Eventually, I couldn't keep pretending everything was okay. Suddenly, I felt like I was walking around with a neon sign flashing my shame. After all, I had stayed, and somehow, I believed that made me less than.

At my best friend's son's wedding, far from home and surrounded by strangers, I felt like myself again, unburdened by the weight of my story. When someone joked that a guest was flirting with me, I laughed it off. Later, it echoed in my mind. Could someone really see me that way? That small comment unlocked something I hadn't felt in a long time: maybe I was still desirable. Maybe I was enough.

Isaiah 32:17 reminds me that true peace and confidence come not from perfection, but from righteousness and trusting in Christ. God created me in His image, which means I was never lacking. My ex-husband's betrayal wasn't a reflection of my worth. It was his sin, not my shortcoming. When I brought my brokenness to God, He didn't just comfort me; He reminded me of who I am.

I don't know if that guy at the wedding was truly flirting with me. What mattered was the idea that someone might. That spark has grown, and today, it shines in my reclaimed confidence.

"And the effect of righteousness will be peace; and the result of righteousness, quietness and confidence forever."

Isaiah 32:17

Made For More

I know who I am 'cause I know who You are
The cross of salvation was only the start
Now I am chosen, free and forgiven
I have a future and it's worth the living

Born and raised back to life again
I was made for more

Josh Baldwin

(Wiggins, Early, Smith, & Baldwin, 2025)

Reflection

When has your outward confidence masked inner pain or insecurity?

What does it mean to you to find confidence through your faith rather than through external validation?

What steps can you take to continue reclaiming your confidence today?

How are you feeling today?

S ☐

M ☐

T ☐

W ☐

T ☐

F ☐

S ☐

Weekly Prayer

Lord, Thank You for reminding me that my worth is found in You. Restore my confidence, quiet my doubts, and help me walk boldly in Your truth. Let Your peace guide me as I rediscover who I am in You—loved, chosen, and enough. Amen.

Laughing More

Laughter offers us a number of gifts. It lightens our stress, lifts our mood, and draws us closer to others. It sparks the release of endorphins, those natural "feel-good" chemicals that soothe pain and heighten joy. When we laugh together, we create moments of connection, a shared joy that strengthens our bonds and adds lightness to even the heaviest days.

And let's be honest—it just feels good.

I met my college roommates in 1985. Two of us lived together, and the other two were across the hall. While we often joke that the college housing office deserves the credit, we're convinced God orchestrated our meeting.

Since then, we've celebrated birthdays, weddings, babies, and now grandbabies. We have mourned and cried together. But mostly, we have shared a million laughs. Sometimes, it's just remembering our dorm antics of loud music, silly dancing and the boys on 1st Floor Tabb. It's remembering the lesson from the plumber's daughter during our our 40th birthday celebration in Disney (FYI, walking away will not stop an overflowing toilet.) or a girl's weekend that always includes Shrimp Dip, shopping, and games. And there is always laughing.

Most recently, they showed up for me in a way they never had to before, but I wasn't surprised. They've been there from the beginning: sometimes with a text, sometimes in phone calls, and sometimes driving hours just to meet me for lunch. They've prayed over me when we're together and when we aren't. Those texts, calls, lunches, and prayers feed my soul. We've had our fair-share of tears and anger and honest conversation. But they always include laughing.

Laughter is medicine to the heart and soul.

Psalm 126 reminds us that joy and laughter are natural responses when we remember all the good things God has done. Even in life's lowest valleys, when we pause to reflect on His faithfulness, we can find ourselves smiling, maybe even laughing, because we know we are deeply loved and never alone. To the girls from 3rd Floor French, you're the best!

"Our mouths were filled with laughter, our tongues with songs of joy. Then it was said among the nations, 'The Lord has done great things for them.'"

Psalm 126:2

I've Got Joy

He gave me beauty from ashes,
turn my life around
He broke my chains
and now I'm dancing on solid ground
For all he has done to save me
I will raise my voice
I've got Jesus so I've got joy

Cece Winans
(Lee & Wickham, 2022)

Reflection

When was the last time you laughed so hard you cried? What made that moment so special?

How has laughter helped you navigate difficult seasons in your life, especially during times of grief or transition?

How can you intentionally invite more laughter and joy into your everyday life, even in the midst of challenges?

What are you grateful for this week?

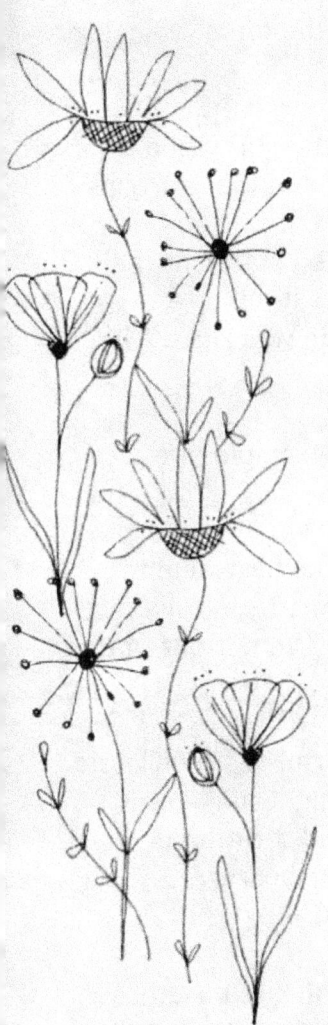

Weekly Prayer

Lord, Thank You for the gift of laughter that lifts our spirits and connects our hearts. Help us remember Your goodness, even in hard times, and find joy in the people and moments You've placed in our lives. Fill our days with light, laughter, and gratitude. Amen.

Gratitude in the Small Things

Having a heart for gratitude is difficult when you feel like everything in your life has changed. When nothing seems the same or you feel tested at each step, being thankful doesn't soar to the top of your list.

In 2004, I was moving into a new classroom, and I elected to move all my things myself. After dozens of trips back and forth with a 7- and 10-year-old in tow, I was exhausted. During one of the last trips a box of posters and classroom decorations fell off the cart and exploded into the hallway outside my classroom. As I stared at the mess, my 7-year-old said, "Man, isn't that great that it fell outside your classroom door and not in the parking lot?" He was right. The parking lot was messy and gravelly and HOT.

It was a stunning lesson in gratitude and a perfect example of a grateful heart.

We might have a mess to clean up, but maybe it's the best time to clean it. For me, I don't have small children at home. I can take care of myself. I have friends and family supporting me. I'm not out in the gravel.

There is so much to be thankful for, even in the storm. It's the classic illustration of filling a jar with large rocks and calling it full—until you add smaller rocks, then pebbles, and finally sand. Gratitude works the same way: it's the little things that fill our hearts completely.

When we can truly be grateful and give thanks "in all circumstances," we find ourselves focusing on the good stuff. Gratitude in the small things helps me fulfill God's will. I am thankful for memes texted to make me giggle. I'm thankful for encouragement videos sent to make me smile. I'm thankful for the friend who helped my boy's pack the moving van and my boy's friends who unpacked it all. I am thankful for walks around the pond at my condo with another friend who lets me vent. Thankful that God put each of these friends in my path.

Today I'm thankful for a warm slice of coffee cake, a quiet morning, my best friend's text, and a working washing machine. Having a feeling of gratitude can keep our focus where it should be, creating a new life that reflects what God wants for us and what we need.

> *"Give thanks in all circumstances;*
> *for this is God's will for you in Christ Jesus."*
>
> 1 Thessalonians 5:18

Thank You Isn't Enough

Thank You for the that air I'm breathing
Thank You for a life full of meaning
Thank You for a brand-new start
A broken heart that's finally beating

For all You've done, got a million reasons
Thank You isn't enough for this kind of love

Tasha Layton
& The Choir Room
(Cates, Jackson, Smith, Layton, 2025)

Reflection

What are three small things you are grateful for today that you might have overlooked a year ago?

Can you recall a time when a difficult moment revealed an unexpected blessing?

Why do you think it's easier to focus on big blessings instead of the small, everyday ones?

How are you feeling today?

S ☐

M ☐

T ☐

W ☐

T ☐

F ☐

S ☐

Weekly Prayer

Lord, when I feel weary and ready to surrender, remind me that You are fighting for me. Calm my anxious heart, steady my spirit, and help me rest in Your strength. Thank You for standing beside me in every battle and guiding me toward peace and victory. Amen.

Don't Give Up

I hate to talk about the legal aspect of a divorce because it feels so sterile, but here goes. Legally, divorce is about assets and debts, dividing and allocating, and breaking down and finalizing. It involves people who are paid to be "on your side" and "fight for you" and can feel hollow.

Even with a lawyer, paperwork, and a court date, the fight that mattered most wasn't in a courtroom. It was a quiet, internal fight to keep going, to stay kind, and to remain grounded. I was determined to not give up on myself or my future.

The legal part might be emotionless, but my reality was anything but that. I was flooded with emotions. There were days I wanted to scream and days I wanted to sleep through it all. Divorce never comes as quickly as we hope, it often feels like it will never end. Frustrations can bubble up as we try to keep things civil.

We want to pack the courtroom, figuratively or physically, with our people firmly on our side. We want people we can count on. Luckily, I had many people who were willing to be there for me. A friend who has been through divorce herself sent me this text:

Tell me the day and time. You won't be alone!

But Exodus 14:14 asks us to think about it a different way: *"The Lord will fight for you; just stay calm."* This verse is not presented as a battle cry, but as an assuring whisper. It taps us on the shoulder and says, "You don't have to gather your troops, God has it. Stay calm."

Calm didn't mean passive. It meant rooted. It meant remembering that God wasn't absent from this mess, He was in it with me. While the world told me to armor up, God told me to hand it over.

If you're in the thick of it, overwhelmed by the cold logistics and heavy emotions, don't give up. You are not alone. You don't have to carry it all or solve it all.

Remember: God is always working behind the scenes for your good. He wouldn't leave you to fight alone. When you walk in faith, you won't have to fight every battle alone.

> *"The Lord will fight for you; Just stay calm."*
>
> Exodus 14:14

I Believe You

I'd be lying if I said that I'm okay
'Cause right now, I'm lost
And lost count of the broken prayers I've prayed
And it's true that some days
It'd be easier to doubt
But Your word has never let me down

So I believe You
When You say You're fighting for me

Megan Woods
(Wedgeworth, Hulse & Woods, 2025)

Reflection

When have you felt like giving up, and how did God remind you He was still fighting for you?

How can you hand your battles over to God instead of carrying them yourself?

Who has reminded you of God's presence when you felt alone in your fight?

What are you grateful for this week?

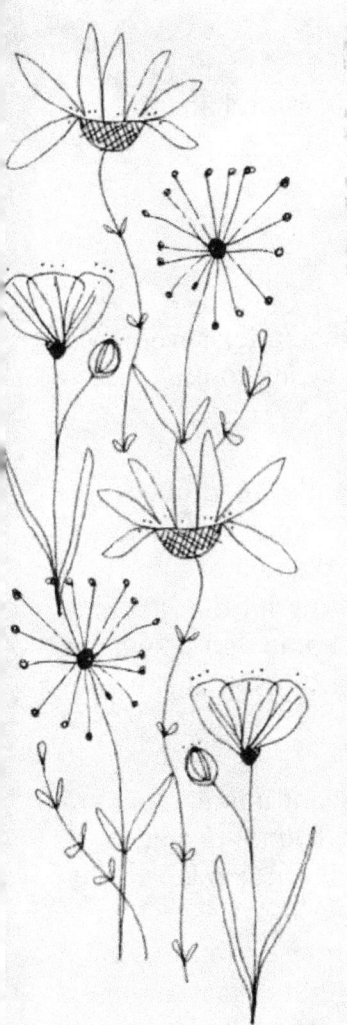

Weekly Prayer

Lord, open my eyes to the small blessings that surround me each day. Help me to give thanks, even in the mess, and to trust that You are working in all things. Let gratitude shape my heart and guide my steps as I walk this new path with You. Amen.

Redefining My Comfort Zone

We love our comfort zone. It's like a big stretched out sweatshirt or a pair of fluffy slippers. It's sitting in my parents living room or beside my sister on the beach. It's called a comfort zone because we feel safe there, even if it's no longer good for us. It is why I stayed in my marriage, because not being in my marriage was just too hard to think about...until it wasn't.

Going out of your comfort zone is basically what divorce is. Our comfort zone is not just deleted, it's obliterated.

I had been very cautious about posting on social media for several months after my separation. I didn't *really* want anyone to ask questions because I didn't *really* have nice, neat answers.

Then, 9 months later, I was eating dinner with friends when one friend noticed a picture on my cellphone. He asked what that picture was, and I told him it was my *unstuck* picture. I explained to him I liked how I looked that day and wanted to remind myself that I could do hard things. He said, "Girl, then you should go home and take a picture of yourself tonight because you look *way* better tonight than in that picture."

I was taken aback. But you know what, I did it. I went home, took the picture, sent it to him and told him thank you. Then, I posted it on Facebook and Instagram unapologetically. And it felt good.

God wants us to come out of our comfort zone to praise him. Joshua 1:9 says, "Be strong and courageous." We want to think that verse is for big stuff, but it's also for the little stuff that seems really big at the time. It's the courage to post a picture, just because someone tells you you look good.

Just because something used to give us comfort doesn't mean it always will. We are allowed to change what brings us comfort. We are allowed to say, "This may have felt good at one time, but it doesn't anymore."

Joshua assures me God is with me wherever I go, and I can always find comfort in Him. Being strong and courageous is always a good option for living life.

> *"Have I not commanded you? Be strong and courageous. Do not be frightened, and do not be dismayed, for the Lord your God is with you wherever you go."*
>
> Joshua 1:9

Build A Boat

You're the map, You're my compass
You help me navigate the currents underneath
Take the lead, I surrender

I will build a boat in the sand
where they say it never rains
I will stand up in faith,
I'll do anything it takes

Colton Dixon

(Mosley, Dixon, Cavazza, Lindbrant, Gormley, 2023)

Reflection

What is one place or situation that used to bring you comfort but no longer serves you well?

Can you recall a time when doing something small, like posting a photo, took big courage?

Like building a boat in the desert, in what ways can you invite God into your moments of bravery?

How are you feeling today?

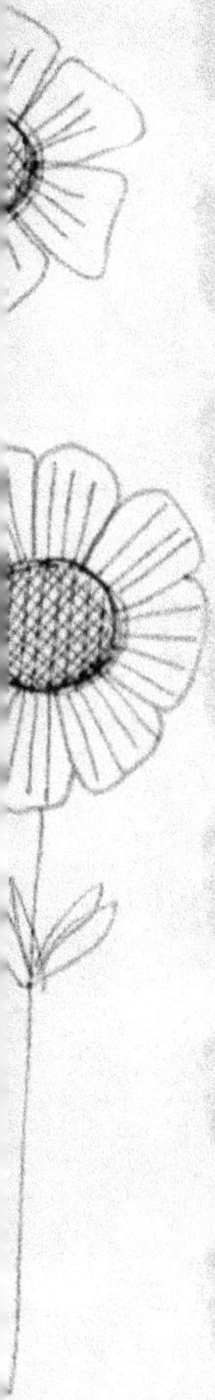

S ☐

M ☐

T ☐

W ☐

T ☐

F ☐

S ☐

Weekly Prayer

Lord, When I feel afraid or unsure, remind me You are already there—strong, steady, and faithful. Help me release the past, embrace the unknown, and trust that Your comfort is greater than anything I leave behind.
Amen.

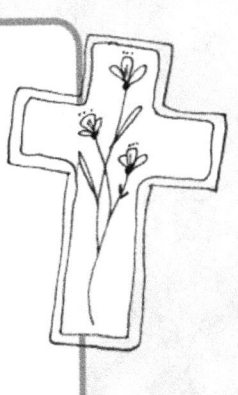

Reclaiming My Peace

I am a beach girl.

I live an hour north of the Outer Banks in North Carolina. Starting with childhood vacations, the Outer Banks is almost a part of who I am. There is something about driving over the Wright Memorial Bridge that lowers my blood pressure, steadies my breathing, and allows me to exhale completely. When I'm at the beach, I sleep deeper. I feel better. The Outer Banks is also beautifully situated on a barrier island, so you can watch the sunrise on the beach and the sunset on the Albemarle Sound. Even at 58, I love playing in the water and jumping with the waves.

What if His peace is like the beach? What if we could breathe better, sleep better, think better, and live better in His peace? Wouldn't we accept His gift without hesitation?

Several times between separation and divorce I found myself driving south. I needed a few hours, a night or several nights to connect with peace. I walked on the beach, sat in the sand, gazed at the sunrise and marveled at the sunset. I prayed for healing and peace.

You can, too. Reclaim your peace, even if your peace isn't found at the beach. Is it a mountaintop covered in snow? Is it a quiet boat ride on a still lake? Is it cooking in your kitchen? Is it reading in a cozy nook by a roaring fire?

It doesn't matter where it is, breathe deep and enjoy it. I think that's exactly what Jesus was offering His disciples in John 14:27: "Peace, I leave with you; My peace I give to you. I do not give to you as the world gives." Jesus wasn't offering temporary peace. He was offering His peace, an undeniable, unshakeable peace that is bigger than anything the world can provide.

God's peace isn't tied to a place. It doesn't require a passport or a plane ticket. His peace is freely given to those who ask. It's breathing calmly, sleeping freely, thinking clearly, and so much more.

God's peace transcends location, circumstances, and even emotions.

No sand required.

"Peace, I leave with you; my peace I give to you. I do not give to you as the world gives. Do not let your hearts be troubled and do not be afraid."

John 14:27

Come As You Are

So lay down your burdens
Lay down your shame
All who are broken
Lift up your face
Oh, wanderer come home
You're not too far
Lay down your hurt lay down your heart
Come as you are

Crowder

(Glover, Crowder & Maher, 2014)

Reflection

When and where do you feel most at peace?

What does it mean to you that God's peace is not tied to a place or circumstance?

When you hear or say "Peace be with you" in church, do you genuinely receive or extend that peace?

What are you grateful for this week?

Weekly Prayer

Lord, Thank You for the peace only You can give. Help me to release fear, quiet my heart, and rest in Your presence. Remind me that Your peace isn't found in a place, but in You. Let me receive it fully—and pass it freely. Amen.

Setting Boundaries

2 Corinthians 6:14 uses the metaphor of a yoke, a wooden beam that joins two oxen to plow together, to explain partnership. Many of us have heard the phrase "equally yoked," which reflects the hope that our closest relationships are built with unity, shared purpose, and mutual investment. While Paul's instruction in this scripture is often interpreted in the context of marriage, the principle can extend to any close relationship, business, friendship, or family, where values are misaligned.

While we are called to love and respect everyone, Paul's message here is about who we deeply connect ourselves to. People in our lives can help our walk with Christ and sadly, sometimes they can hinder our walk. Healthy boundaries help you protect your values when others are living in ways that contradict them. It's not about judgment. It's about wisdom, clarity, and spiritual protection.

When you set a boundary that honors God, you are trusting Him more than your own comfort or fear of disappointing others. Setting boundaries grounded in faith doesn't always come easily, especially when emotions and history are involved. I've had to learn this firsthand.

Early in the separation, I decided my ex would not visit my new home. I needed this space to be a sanctuary, free from stress and fully my own. Although Christmas looked different that year, it was a peaceful kind of different. I wasn't guarded. I simply enjoyed being present with my children on that special day.

As the separation continued, I needed to block him from texting me. Blocking him felt like an emotional necessity. I needed to protect my peace and avoid the emotional disruption of a surprise message. I explained this to my boys, and they understood the boundary was both reasonable and necessary.

Boundaries aren't just about people. They are about peace and growth. I have also had conversations with a dear friend about keeping a personal boundary with relationships until I am ready for deeper connections. For now, boundaries are about protecting myself.

Setting and keeping healthy boundaries is an act of faith and courage.

> *"Do not be yoked together with unbelievers. For what do righteousness and wickedness have in common? Or what fellowship can light have with darkness?"*
>
> 2 Corinthians 6:14

I draw a permanent boundary line
The enemy has no rights
To come near my family
No scheme could ever undo God's plans
No matter the circumstance
The cross has sealed my destiny

Hope Darst
& The Becoming Co.
(Sooter, Darst, & Sloat, 2024)

Reflection

What boundaries in your life have been the hardest to set? Why?

How do you know when a boundary is rooted in faith rather than fear or control?

What has God shown you about honoring Him through the boundaries you've established?

How are you feeling today?

S ☐

M ☐

T ☐

W ☐

T ☐

F ☐

S ☐

Weekly Prayer

Lord, give me strength to set boundaries that honor You. Help me choose peace over pressure and clarity over confusion. When it's hard to let go, remind me I'm walking toward Your purpose. Protect my heart and guide my steps with wisdom, grace, and courage. Amen.

When Worries Abound

Sadly, my story isn't unique. Yes, there are nuances that belong to only me. My details may be different from your details, but the result is not unique. I was betrayed.

When I was confronted with proof of betrayal, I realized my instincts were right. The betrayal ran deep. Unfortunately, betrayal doesn't just break your heart; it breaks your confidence, your soul, and your sense of safety. Then, worry temporarily fills the gaps.

At the beginning of the separation, worry filled my every thought. Though I knew leaving was the only path for me, I had so much worry about the impact my decision had on my sons and my parents, about financial matters and about my future living arrangements.

Additionally, when betrayal includes infidelities, you worry about your health and your body. There is nothing more humbling than going to my doctor at 58-years-old and asking for tests about my body, but I had to do it. Thankfully all the tests came back clear.

In the middle of my worry, this verse from 1 Peter became my anchor. 1 Peter says, "cast all your anxiety on Him." He will never betray you. He will only be there to collect your worries when you rely on Him. This felt overwhelming. My anxiety didn't feel like something I could hand over. It was tangled in every decision, every sleepless night, and every "what if" scenario I was experiencing. However, the verse continues with "because He cares for you." He cares in a way that is active, present, and constant. God isn't indifferent to your pain. He's not disappointed in your worry. He wants to carry it for you.

He didn't erase the pain, but he sat with me through it. He gave me moments of peace in the chaos. He whispered reminders that I was still His; still whole in His eyes and still worthy of love and protection.

Casting my anxiety on Him didn't mean the worry disappeared overnight. It meant I stopped carrying it alone. There is a quote stating, "Worry is a conversation you have with yourself about things you cannot change, But prayer is a conversation you have with God about things that He can change."

> *"Cast all your anxiety on Him
> because he cares for you."*
>
> 1 Peter 5:7

The God Who Stays

You're the God who stays
You're the one who runs in my direction
When the whole world walks away
You're the God who stands
With wide open arms
And You tell me nothing
I have ever done can separate my heart
From the God who stays

Matthew West
(West, Pruis, and Smith, 2019)

Reflection

What worries have felt too heavy for you to "cast" onto God, and what might it look like to start releasing them?

Can you think of a time when prayer shifted your perspective, even if your circumstances didn't change?

What practical steps could help you turn worry into prayer this week?

What are you grateful for this week?

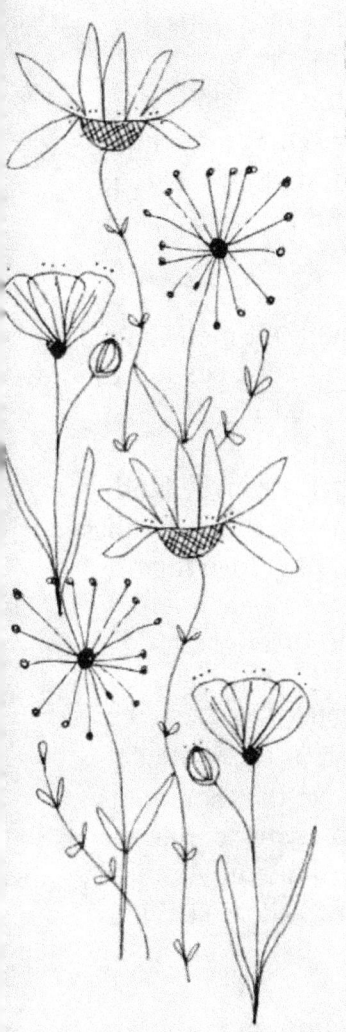

Weekly Prayer

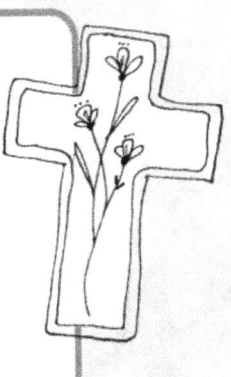

Heavenly Father, when worries weigh heavy and fears consume my thoughts, remind me that You care deeply for me. Help me release each burden into Your hands. Replace my anxious heart with peace and my restless mind with trust. Amen.

Accepting Compliments

James reminds us that every good and perfect gift comes from God. During the year of my separation, I learned that even small moments, like kind words from another person, can be among those gifts.

There were a lot of "firsts" in the year of separation. The first time you buy groceries for yourself or the first time you go to a wedding by yourself seem monumental. Then there's the firsts that feel weird: the first time someone compliments you and the first time someone asks you out on a date.

To be fair, my ex was very complimentary. He would tell me I looked nice or tell me how he was proud of me, but when his words didn't match his actions, I didn't believe the compliments were real.

Hearing a compliment from a friend or even relative stranger lands differently, too. But, accepting compliments is something that honors God. He made us in His image. Compliments reflect his love for us. Honoring that, when someone told me I looked good or seemed brighter, I simply said, "Thank you" or "Thank you, I *feel* good."

Someone else said to me, "Man, you radiate positivity." Now, that's a compliment! I want to be a better version of myself at the end of this. I want to remain positive about the future, and I love that someone could feel positivity from me. During the separation, your confidence can take a hit, and you can get down on yourself. Allowing yourself to take compliments from others helps you see how others see you and it feels good.

Make sure you take the time to acknowledge the compliment by simply saying "Thank you." Recognize God's role in providing you with the gifts someone sees. Don't deflect or diminish the compliment. Allow yourself to believe it. If someone is complimenting something that is clearly a gift from God, acknowledge God's role in that either out loud or in a quiet prayer.

James 1:17 is about us! We should be proud to be a child of God. Receiving a compliment is a reminder that God's light is shining through us. It's a reminder that we are His creation, one of His good and perfect gifts.

> *"Every good and perfect gift is from above, coming down from the Father of the heavenly lights, who does not change like shifting shadows."*
>
> James 1:17

House of the Lord

We worship the God who was
We worship the God who is
We worship the God who evermore will be
He opened the prison doors
He parted the raging sea
My God, He holds the victory
There's joy in the house of the Lord

Phil Wickham
(Smith & Wickham, 2021)

Reflection

Why do you think it's often harder to believe compliments from others than it is to believe criticism?

How does accepting a compliment honor God and reflect His image in us?

How can you remind yourself that a compliment is a reflection of God's goodness in you rather than pride?

How are you feeling today?

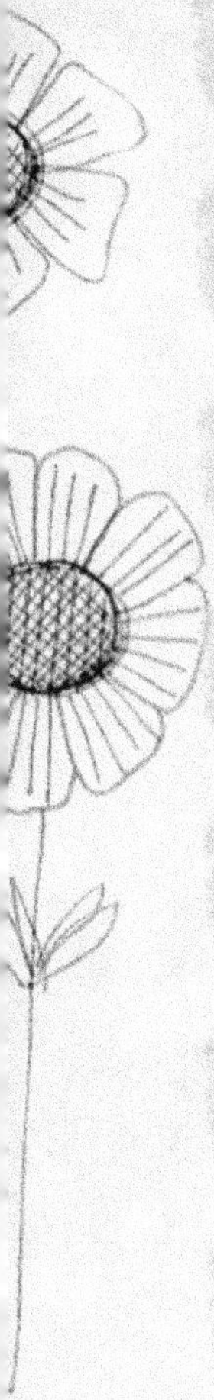

S ☐

M ☐

T ☐

W ☐

T ☐

F ☐

S ☐

Weekly Prayer

Heavenly Father, Thank You for the kind words You send through others. Help me to receive compliments with grace and humility, seeing them as reminders of Your goodness in me. Teach me to honor You by shining Your light in all I do. Amen.

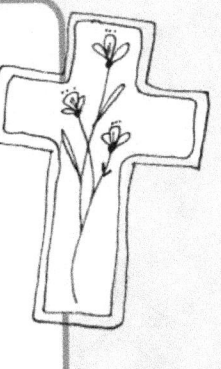

Finding The Joy

One day I was talking to my therapist about feeling stuck. I was telling her I felt like my life was on hold. I knew I had made progress, but I felt like I was stuck in between being married and being single and I wasn't sure who I was. That day, she told me about GLAD (Gratitude, Learning, Accomplishment, and Delight). I discussed this in better detail in the section on Asking for Help. When she said, "Delight in the Lord and find your joy," I burst into tears. She was as surprised as I was at my reaction.

When I got myself together, I showed her my wrist. I have a small tattoo with my mother-in-law's initials and angel wings.

I loved my mother-in-law. In 2021, I had the honor and privilege of sitting with her while she was in hospice in Ohio. Thankfully, my sister-in-law lived nearby, and I stayed with her.

Each day after coming home from the hospital, I would ask my sister-in-law, "What is our joy today?" I knew we needed to "find the joy" in this period. We reveled in the joy that she spoke to each grandchild on a video call before she slipped into unconsciousness. We celebrated joy when we learned she left detailed plans for her passing and service, so no one had to make a million decisions in the middle of mourning. We celebrated joy that she lived long enough that Covid restrictions were lifted in her church, and we could invite lots of people to celebrate her life. We found joy that she passed quietly with her oldest daughter and oldest granddaughter in the room. Though I hadn't walked this path before, I knew God had my hand. He had directed my question of the day, and He is the one that reminded me there's always joy to be found.

Flash forward, when my therapist told me I should "find the joy" it struck me as a God moment, reminding me, once again, He had my hand. It was my mantra then; it has become my mantra now.

What is your joy today? A warm bed? A peaceful cup of coffee? A cozy chair in front of the fire? A win with the lawyer? A walk around the park?

We can always find joy in every situation.

> "Let the trees of the forest sing, let them sing for joy before the Lord, for He comes to judge the earth."
>
> 1 Chronicles 16:33

Can't Steal My Joy

In the high highs, in the low lows
You fill my cup, You fill it up until it overflows
I remember, I'll keep holding on to hope
'Cause you're the King of rolling stones

Can't steal my joy

Josiah Queen

(Sooter, Bentley, Lake & Queen, 2025)

Reflection

What does "finding the joy" look like in your current season of life?

Think of a difficult moment in your life—can you identify something joyful that came out of it?

How can you make "finding the joy" a regular practice in your life?

What are you grateful for this week?

Weekly Prayer

Lord, in every season, help me find the joy You've placed before me. Even in sorrow, remind me You are near. Let gratitude grow in my heart and trust take root in my soul. Thank You for orchestrating beauty even in brokenness. You are my joy. Amen.

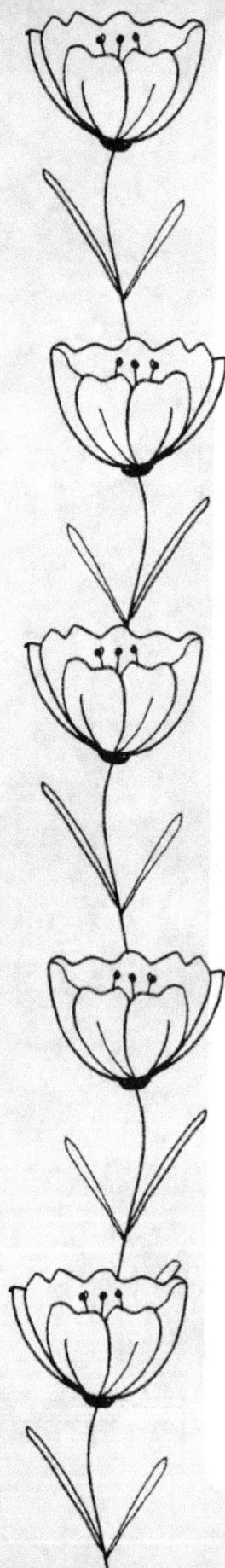

Healing In Nature

Have you ever noticed how being in nature slows us down and makes us breathe? I'll be the first to admit I have a black thumb. I can't keep a plant alive, no matter what. I've tried and tried, but the results are the same. So, when I tell you there is healing in nature, I may seem to be a funny one to trust.

Psalm 23 gives quiet power to nature. Being in nature reminds me I'm part of something bigger and that I don't have to have it all figured out. The green pastures and quiet waters help to refresh my soul.

In my first year of separation, I've told you I took comfort on the beach. However, I also found peace hiking through Saguaro National Park, surrounded by towering cacti that have stood through centuries of storms and scorching sun. I was reminded of resilience and beauty in what could appear to be a barren landscape. Even while sitting by a fire pit on a crisp fall evening, watching sparks float into the night sky, I felt a peace that no "to-do list" could give me. Each place may feel different, but it's all about God's peace.

I am not rushed on the beach or on the hiking trail or by the fire pit.

Nature doesn't strain to be what it is. Flowers don't strain to be flowers. They are what they were created to be. They grow, bloom, and reflect the glory of their Maker. We need to take a cue from nature and rest in God's provision, letting healing happen in its own time. God can turn broken pieces of our hearts or our lives into peace and quiet.

So, I put my toes in the sand.

I sat in the warmth of the sun.

I listened to the quiet of the night sky.

I let nature remind me that I am enough. I was created and molded into who I was meant to be. The green pastures and still waters refresh my soul.

"The Lord is my shepherd, I lack nothing. He makes me lie down in green pastures, He leads me beside quiet waters, he refreshes my soul."

Psalm 23:1-2

153

Still Waters

Still waters run through any valley I could find
I'm laying fear down,
here at Heaven's riverside
Your word has been true in every season of my life

Oh, the Lord is my shepherd, I shall not want
He leads me by still waters 'til my fears are gone

Leanna Crawford
(Richards, Gamble, and Crawford, 2024)

Reflection

When was the last time you felt close to God while in nature? What was that moment like?

Which place—beach, desert, forest, or firelight—feels most healing to you, and why?

How does Psalm 23:1–2 remind you of God's presence in everyday life?

How are you feeling today?

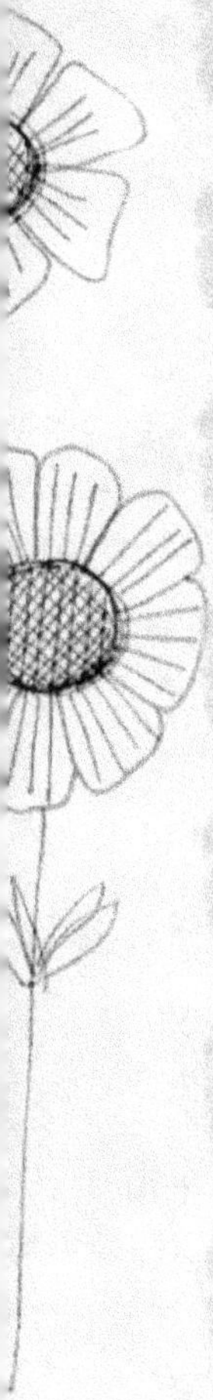

S ☐

M ☐

T ☐

W ☐

T ☐

F ☐

S ☐

Weekly Prayer

Lord, In the sound of waves, the whisper of wind, and the stillness of night, remind me of Your peace. Help me rest in Your care, trusting that, like the wildflowers, I am growing exactly as You designed. Amen.

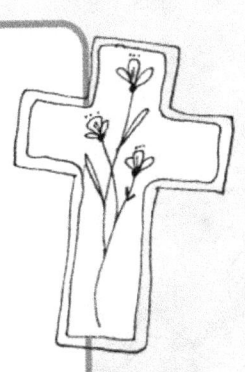

Knowing My Non-Negotiables

I love a good rom-com. I can sit for days and watch one right after another. I can recite key phrases from my favorites, and sigh at all the right lines. I have always wanted to be loved that way. Sadly, we all recognize that rom-coms aren't real. A car wreck resulting in amnesia while being taken in by a handsome man who is a millionaire and owns a pumpkin patch in Vermont probably won't be my path to happiness.

I had lunch with a friend just a few months into my separation and explained how I truly felt God had a hand in my divorce and was working for me. She asked if I was ready to consider dating. "Absolutely not" was my quick response. "How would that work?" "How do I meet someone?" "I don't know how to do that!"

She calmly said, "If you believe God had you in His hands during the divorce, don't you think He'll hold you through that, too?" Sigh. While I still don't know the answers to those questions, this is what I do know.

I do know I don't want to be alone for the rest of my life. I'm only 58. I could live another 30 years and doing it alone seems terrible.

I do know I want someone who has a visible faith; someone who can go to church with me, pray with me, and see the positive side of life.

I do know I want to find someone who will love my children. I know they're grown, but they play an important part in my life, and I want someone who isn't jealous of my relationship with them.

I do know I want someone who is adventurous and willing to travel. I also probably need someone to pull me out of my comfort zone every now and then; and I know that comes with trust. Speaking of which, I need someone I can trust completely. Someone who is honest and wants the best for me.

That being said, I don't want to be hurt again.

So where does that leave me? Am I ready? Romans 8:28 assures me that God's plans for me will be for my good. I need to trust him in every step, even this one.

> *"And we know that in all things God works for the good of those who love Him, who have been called according to His purpose."*
>
> Romans 8:28

A Thousand Times

And every tear that you cried
Every broken prayer you prayed
He turned it for good
He let's nothing go to waste

You can count on that
You know what He's like
You've seen Him do it a thousand times

We Are Messengers
(Mulligan, Hulse & Smith, 2024)

Reflection

What are the non-negotiables for your life moving forward?

Which of your non-negotiables reflects your deepest faith values?

How can you ensure your next relationship allows both people to grow in faith and love?

What are you grateful for this week?

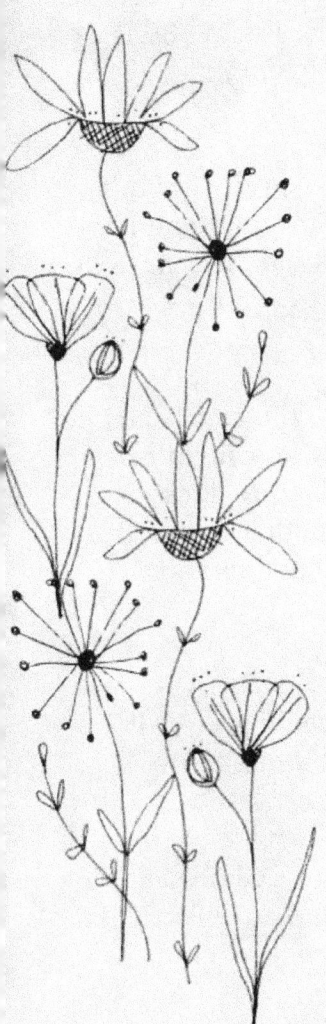

Weekly Prayer

Heavenly Father, Thank You for guiding my heart through loss and healing. Teach me to wait with faith, to love with wisdom, and to believe that all things work for my good through You. Amen.

Owning My Worth

I am "fearfully and wonderfully made." I was intentionally crafted by God Himself. If the Creator of the universe designed me with care, then my value is already secure and unquestionable. Psalm 139 is a reminder that my worth isn't determined by outside opinions, achievements, or comparisons.

For so long I resisted thoughts of divorce because of pride. I didn't want people to know I couldn't keep my marriage together and my husband would seek others outside our marriage. I didn't want to be the first divorce in our friend group. I didn't want to admit I had failed.

I have now come to realize I also devalued myself. I thought I should stay with someone who didn't value me, someone who couldn't be trusted with my heart. My therapist told me that God provides for divorce. Marriage is, in fact, a covenant with one another and God and it's intended to be for life. However, in cases of adultery and abandonment, God allows a divorce.

If we were talking about something tangible, like a valuable vase or coin, we would place it in the safest of spots. We would protect it from harm and even create impenetrable measures around it to ensure its safety. Why wouldn't we do that for ourselves?

Although we are valuable beyond measure, I am sure God doesn't want us to create said impenetrable measures around our hearts. He wants us to be loved. He doesn't want us to be alone.

In the darkest night, ships at sea must rely on a lighthouse to keep them off the rocks. God is that lighthouse. He is keeping us safe and guiding our way. We need to value ourselves enough to follow His light. Value what he has made and keep it safe from those that would harm it spiritually, mentally, or physically.

God made you wonderfully His, He wants the best for you. Hold yourself in high esteem and make yourself available to only those who are worthy.

> *"I praise you, for I am fearfully and wonderfully made. Wonderful are your works; my soul knows it very well."*
>
> Psalm 139:14

God Story

My life is a God story
Gotta tell the world what He's done for me
Miracle on miracles that only He could do
I'm proof that we're all only
one prayer away from a testimony
There's only One getting all the glory
My whole life is a God story

Anne Wilson
(West, Pardo & Wilson, 2025)

Reflection

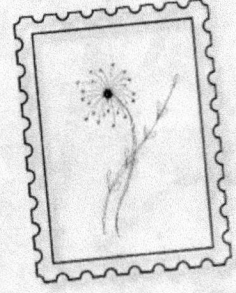

What does it mean to you personally to be "fearfully and wonderfully made"?

When have you allowed others to define your worth instead of God?

How does viewing God as your lighthouse reshape the way you see your future?

How are you feeling today?

S ☐

M ☐

T ☐

W ☐

T ☐

F ☐

S ☐

Weekly Prayer

Lord, remind me daily that I am fearfully and wonderfully made in Your image. Help me to see my value through Your eyes, to guard my heart, and to walk confidently in Your light. Thank You for creating me with purpose and for guiding me toward peace and safety.
Amen.

A Season of Waiting

Waiting isn't fun. No matter the season, we don't like waiting. As children, we don't like waiting on Christmas morning. As teens, we don't like waiting on a college acceptance letter (or email). As adults, we don't like waiting in a doctor's office. And as someone who is separated, we don't like waiting on the divorce decree. I didn't even like waiting for any correspondence from my lawyer. Each email included more edits, different wishes, and more waiting.

The reality is we've created a practice of waiting, and it's never fun! If we're waiting for something exciting our stomach does flip-flops and we are giddy with anticipation. If we are waiting for something bad our stomach does flip-flops, but we are nauseous with anticipation. Waiting in thanksgiving feels different from waiting in a crisis.

What makes waiting bearable? Can there be joy in the waiting? With God, waiting is never wasted. Even when it's hard to worship, we can be real with God. He knows where we are "in the waiting."

Until you are in the middle of the divorce process, you have no idea how much waiting there truly is. I want to believe there is power in waiting. Waiting helps us know exactly what we want and exactly what we need. Waiting helps the healing start. Waiting can also bring us to our knees and maybe that's where God wants us.

I have told friends I felt like I was on the runner's block, crouched and waiting for someone to fire the shot to start my life. My therapist said, "Run. Live your life. Don't pause your life for a life change. God has a plan."

He was working in me while I was waiting. He was building a better me.

I saw a post of social media the other day that said, "Sometimes the wait is longer, because the blessing is bigger." I'll take it.

Just as Proverbs 3 says, we need to trust God has the best plans for us. His path for us awaits. He knows the path we will take, and he knows that path will be best for His children. We must have faith while we are waiting.

> *"Trust in the Lord with all your heart and lean not on your own understanding; in all your ways submit to Him, and He will make your paths straight."*
>
> Proverbs 3:5-6

There was Jesus

In the waiting, in the searching
In the healing and the hurting
Like a blessing buried in the broken pieces
Every minute, every moment
Where I've been and where I'm going
Even when I didn't know it or couldn't see it
There was Jesus

Zach Williams
& Dolly Parton
(Williams, Smith and Beathard, 2019)

Reflection

What areas of your life are you being called to wait in right now?

Have you ever looked back on a season of waiting and recognized God's purpose in it?

When waiting feels unbearable, what practical or spiritual practices help you stay grounded in faith?

What are you grateful for this week?

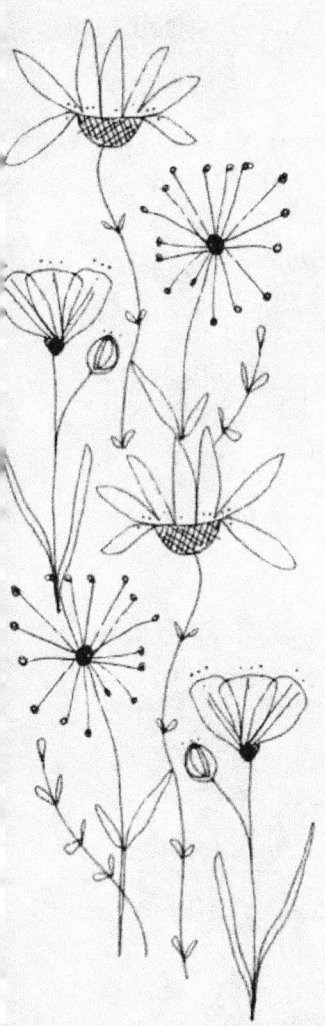

Weekly Prayer

Lord, in this season of waiting, calm my anxious heart. Help me trust You fully, even when I don't understand. Teach me to find peace in Your timing and strength in Your promises. Lead me forward with faith, knowing You are working all things for my good. Amen.

Walking In Purpose

From the moment anyone asked me what I wanted to be when I grew up, the answer was always to become a teacher. I loved getting a chalkboard for Christmas when I was five. No one was surprised I became a teacher.

I retired in 2021 after 31 years of teaching and settled into "retirement" as a full-time professional development presenter. I wrote a book for an educational company about teaching and was excited about the future. I felt like that was my purpose.

Then, in 2024, education was in the middle of a huge shift in ideology, opportunities for working with teachers started shrinking and I felt out of the loop. Interestingly enough, I believed in the shift in education, but I think I was looked at as an "old dog" in a world full of "new tricks."

And then, to top it off, I left my marriage.

2024 was the year my world shifted, and my purpose was shaken. I wasn't sure where I fit in the world of education, and I wasn't sure where I fit in a world of married friends.

The only unshakable thing at this time was my faith in God. My faith grew and strengthened each day.

Ephesians 2 states we are His great handiwork, created by Him to do good works, which he has prepared in advance for us to do. All three sections of that verse are powerful. We are His "handiwork." He made me. He made me a teacher, a talker, and a leader. We are created "to do good works." I am anxious for what God has in store for me. He knows what my talents are, and He knows how to use me for his "good works." Finally, he "prepared in advance" for me. He knows the struggles and the triumphs. He knows the good, the bad and the ugly. He knew all along that my journey would lead me to His purpose.

With so much uncertainty in going through a divorce, it is surprising how calm I am about not fully knowing His purpose for me. I think that's my strongest admission of faith yet. I am fully committed and walking in His purpose as it is revealed to me.

> "For we are God's handiwork, created in Christ Jesus to do good works, which God prepared in advance for us to do."
>
> Ephesians 2:10

God's Not Done With You

God's not done with you
Even with your broken heart
and your wounds and your scars
God's not done with you
Even when you're lost
and it's hard and you're falling apart
God's not done with you
It's not over, it's only begun

Tauren Wells

(Herms Weisband, & Wells, 2017)

Reflection

How has your understanding of "purpose" changed throughout different seasons of your life?

In what ways has God used your gifts, even when your path looked uncertain?

What "good works" do you feel God has prepared for you right now?

How are you feeling today?

S ☐

M ☐

T ☐

W ☐

T ☐

F ☐

S ☐

Weekly Prayer

Heavenly Father, Thank You for creating me with purpose and intention. Help me walk boldly in faith, trusting that every step leads closer to the purpose You designed for me. Amen.

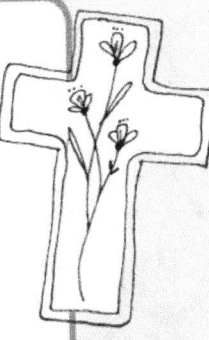

A Beautiful Life

I heard Pat Barrett's song "Beautiful Life" on the radio. It's one of those songs you can't help but turn up and sing loudly. It has the feeling of an 80's rock band concert with an echo chant of sorts. I feel like I could get a bunch of women together and we'd have one arm in the air, waving to the beat.

In the midst of the yuck that is separation, finding the beauty can be hard. We find ourselves looking for the bad and being afraid of the unknown. Thankfully, an anthem like "Beautiful Life" reminds us of all the beauty in our lives.

I met my parents for lunch the other day. They are getting older, and I know these days are to be cherished. It's a beautiful life.

My boys are amazing. Really. I know I talk about them all the time, but their support and encouragement is unbelievable. The other day they were over with their significant others for brunch and to fix my garage door opener. Afterwards, we all sat at the pool. It's a beautiful life.

My sister is my best friend. She is ready to fight for me or cheer for me in a moment's notice. It's a beautiful life.

My sister's granddaughter is the sweetest little 3-year-old. We absolutely spoil her, but I feel like that's our job. This little girl always has a hug and a smile for me. It's a beautiful life.

I could continue to list my people, but you get the idea. It's a beautiful life.

Even in the midst of the not-so-beautiful, it is a beautiful life. There are days it's easier to find the sadness and the doubt, but we need to walk the harder path and find the beauty. Somedays the beautiful might be hidden, but it's there.

Ecclesiastes reminds us God planned this beautiful day. He planned a beautiful life for all of us. We have to remember that. So, put your right hand up and sway to the beat. "Oh, what a beautiful life, oh, what a beautiful life."

> "He has made everything beautiful in its time.
> He has also set eternity in the human heart;
> yet no one can fathom what God has
> done from beginning to end."
>
> Ecclesiastes 3:11

Beautiful Life

Every day is a gift from God
Even ones that have left their scars

Oh, what a beautiful life
What a time to be alive
It doesn't mean it's always gonna feel alright
But it'll be a gift if you hold it right
Oh, what a beautiful life

Pat Barrett

(Johnson, Barrett, Price & Davenport, 2024)

Reflection

What moments in your daily life remind you that it's truly a "beautiful life"?

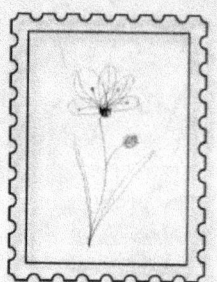

Who are the people God has placed in your life to make it more beautiful?

How do you recognize God's hand in both ordinary and extraordinary moments?

What are you grateful for this week?

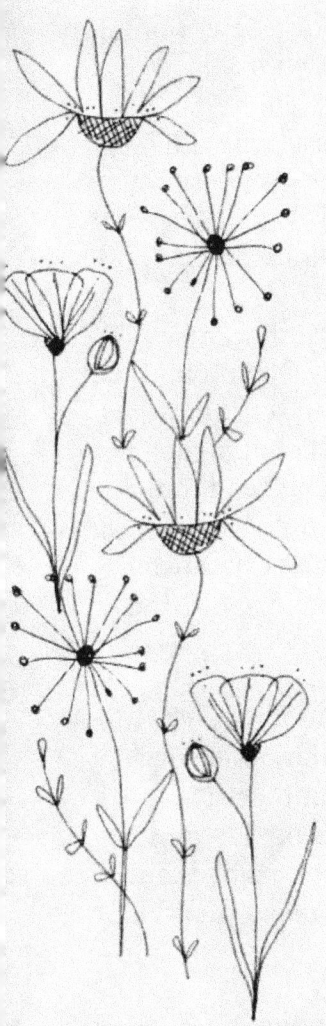

Weekly Prayer

Lord, Thank You for the beauty You weave through every season of my life. Help me see Your hand in both joy and struggle, and to cherish the people You've placed around me. Truly, You've made everything beautiful in its time. Amen.

See Mountains Move

As the year of separation wears on, it wears on you. In Virginia, for a no-fault divorce when you have no minor children, you have to be separated for 6 months and have a signed spousal agreement on file to be divorced. I thought that would be the case. It wasn't.

It was harder to reach an agreement than I thought it would be, and my ex didn't get a lawyer until 6 months after I did. We were separated for thirteen months before an agreement was reached. It was thirteen months of uncertainty, wondering, and unknown.

Although I knew God had a hand in my separation and in my decision, it's easy to forget when the months linger. One night, I had come down with a nasty stomach bug and was by myself. Don't get me wrong, I don't want to be coddled when I'm sick, but somehow it seemed lonelier knowing that no one would pop their head into my room to check on me or ask if I needed anything. I did reach out to my oldest son and ask him to bring me a bottle of Coke because I was raised to believe saltine crackers and a real Coke could fix any stomach issue.

While I was laying on the couch for the what felt like the 100th hour, I was watching an inspirational movie. The father-in-law was speaking to a son-in-law about his sick daughter. He said, "Faith isn't sometimes, it's all the time. Faith isn't second guessing; it's praying and expecting a blessing." It hit me like a ton of bricks. I had faith, but I was second guessing; not second guessing the separation but second guessing the blessing.

How can I have faith in a decision I know, without a doubt, was made possible by God, and not believe he would work to my benefit? I can't have faith in some things and not all things. Matthew 17:20 reminds us we don't have to have a trunk load of faith; we just need enough faith to fit in a mustard seed. AND faith can move mountains.

The year that was my separation took a toll on my faith. My faith may have waned, but it never disappeared. Some days it may have felt small enough for that mustard seed, but that's ok.

I stopped second-guessing. He is in charge. He is the blessing.

> *"Because you have so little faith. Truly I tell you, if you have faith as small as a mustard seed, you can say to this mountain, 'Move from here to there,' and it will move. Nothing will be impossible for you."*
>
> Matthew 17:20

Somebody Prayed

When you're wondering if He's hearing you
Look at me, I'm living proof
I'm only right where I am today
Because somebody prayed

These hands have no power
But there ain't an hour He don't come through
That's why when mountains move, I say
"Looks like somebody prayed"

Crowder

(Crowder, Glover, Sokja, & Cochren, 2024)

Reflection

What "mountains" in your life have seemed too big to move, and how has your faith helped you face them?

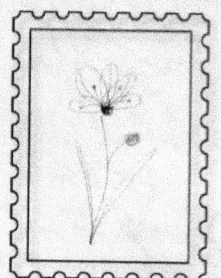

Can you recall a time when your faith felt as small as a mustard seed but still brought peace or progress?

How do you remind yourself that God is working behind the scenes even when you can't see results?

How are you feeling today?

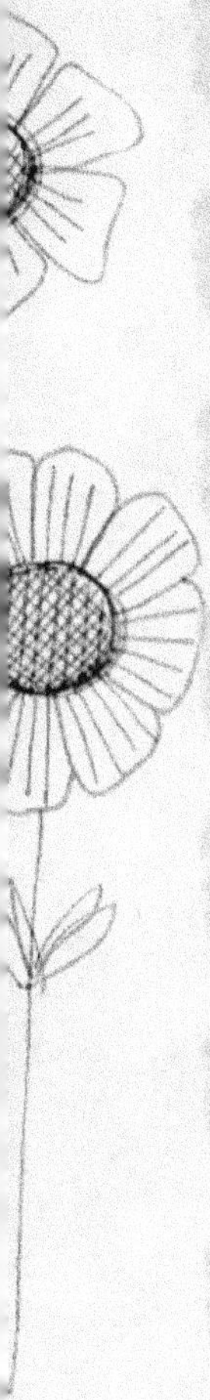

S ☐

M ☐

T ☐

W ☐

T ☐

F ☐

S ☐

Weekly Prayer

Lord, when my faith feels small, remind me that even mustard seed faith can move mountains. Help me trust You fully—in sickness, waiting, and uncertainty. Strengthen my heart to believe in Your blessings, even when I can't see them. Amen.

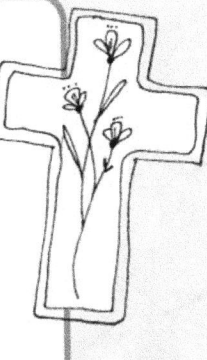

Owning My Story

For the last 10 years I did everything I could to NOT tell my story. I pretended to the world that my marriage was good. In September of 2024, my biggest goal was keeping my divorce quiet until we found the "right time" to tell our sons we would be divorcing. From that moment on, I struggled to talk about my divorce to anyone outside of my circle.

It wasn't a secret, but I didn't know what to say. My circle was safe. I only had to say it once, to the people I loved, and then we could move on about the business of life. I would occasionally run into someone who knew what was going on (probably from a friend of a friend), and I could talk about the divorce without having to say I was getting divorced.

It seemed awkward to casually drop it into a conversation with someone who was "out of the loop." One of my biggest fears in telling people was that I would get a look of pity from them.

Then, I owned my story.

Almost one year from the day of separation, I ran into an old friend at church. We'd known each other since middle school and have crossed paths over the years.

We hugged and I asked how he was doing. After getting caught up on his life and family, he asked me the same. "Well, this past year has been tough. I'm almost at the finish line of getting a divorce but I'm gonna be ok. God has had a hand in everything."

"Oh goodness, I hadn't heard about that," he said. "I'm so sorry." Our conversation continued for a few more minutes, then we hugged and went our separate ways.

I did it. I owned my story, my way and it felt good! There was a little shock detected, but no pity. Luke 12:12 couldn't have been more real or more present. "For the Holy Spirit will teach you at that time what you should say." And he did.

Owning my story was liberating. Once again, His timing was divine.

> *"For the Holy Spirit will teach you at that time what you should say."*
>
> Luke 12:12

The truth is I am my Father's child
I make Him proud,
and I make Him smile
I was made in the image of a perfect King
He looks at me
and wouldn't change a thing

Megan Woods
(Pardo, West, and Woods, 2024)

Reflection

Why do you think it's so hard to share personal struggles, even with people who care about us?

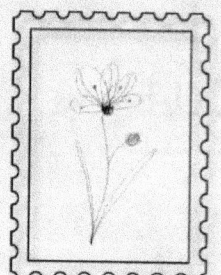

What changes when we stop hiding our pain and begin to tell the truth about our journey?

How can sharing your story become a testimony of God's faithfulness rather than a tale of heartbreak?

What are you grateful for this week?

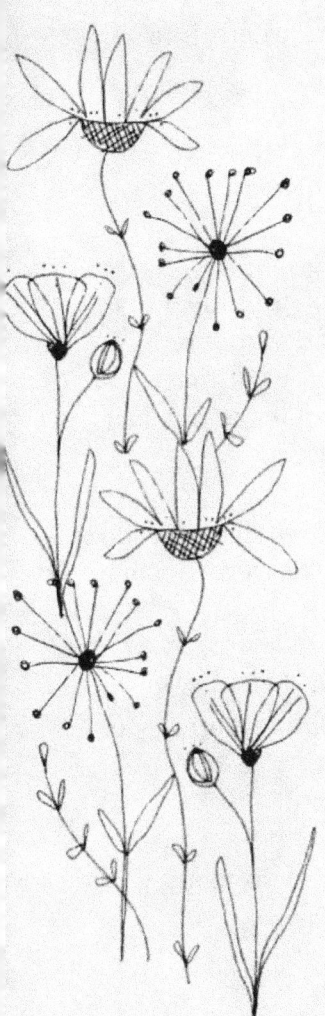

Weekly Prayer

Lord, Thank You for reminding me that my story is Yours too. Give me courage to speak truth with grace and to trust the Holy Spirit to guide my words. May my honesty reflect Your goodness and bring healing—to me and to those who hear my story. Amen.

Faith Over Fear

Amid all the changes and challenges, one truth remains: Life goes on, and time moves forward. While I was creating new routines and learning to live a new life, days turned to weeks and weeks into months.

I was ready for my marriage to come to an end and glad when a meeting was finally on the books between me and my ex and our lawyers. But the date seemed to loom.

No matter how much I've grown over the last year, I could feel my old fears creeping in. When the night came, my mind wandered. What would be the result? Would either of us come out of that meeting feeling triumphant or would we both realize what was lost? Would we even come to a consensus during the meeting?

I understood there wouldn't be a winner and a divorce decree cannot "make things right" or "even a score." I also knew we were closing the door on our life together.

I lived a long time in a marriage that hurt because of fear. I was afraid to leave for so many reasons I've discussed already, afraid to fight because I didn't want to seem weak, and afraid to lose everything.

I am not the same woman I was then. I have grown in so many ways, but mostly I have grown in my faith.

I chose faith over fear.

This doesn't mean I don't get scared. I do. I'm human, but when I do I need to remember Psalm 56.

This verse reminds me that my faith allows me to put my fears in someone else's hands. Because my trust is rooted in my faith, my fears are His and I can be strong.

God has great plans for me, and He has my fear. He will not let me down. No matter how many times I bring my fears to Him, He will take them. I can be free of fear and focus on faith.

> *"When I am afraid, I put my trust in you. In God, whose word I praise, in God I trust and will not be afraid. What can mere mortals do to me?"*
>
> Psalm 56:3-4

No Fear

You might think that I'd be afraid
Runnin' scared with a shaken faith
But the God I know says it ain't over
The God I know is gonna make a way

Yea, though I walk through the valley
I will have No fear
The mighty power of Jesus is fighting for me here

John Reddick

(Reddick, Pardo & West, 2024)

Reflection

What specific fears are hardest for you to hand over to God?

In what ways do you remind yourself to trust God when fear creeps back in?

How can you encourage others who are struggling to choose faith over fear?

How are you feeling today?

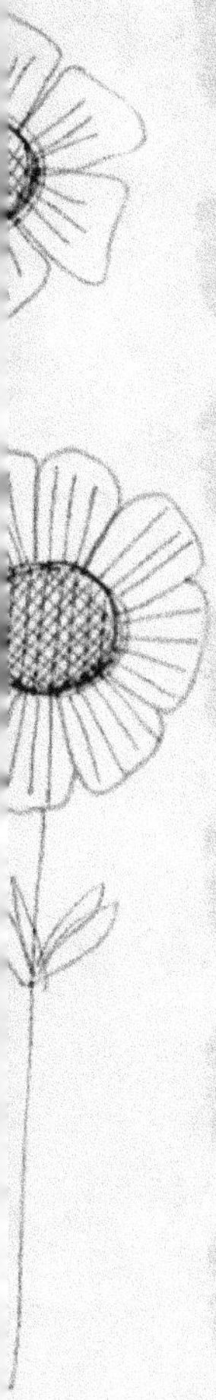

S ☐

M ☐

T ☐

W ☐

T ☐

F ☐

S ☐

Weekly Prayer

Lord, when fear whispers lies and uncertainty clouds my path, remind me to trust You completely. Fill my heart with courage and peace, knowing You walk beside me in every battle. Amen.

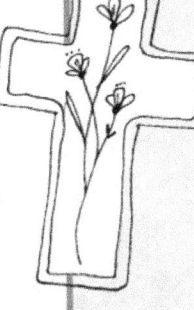

Goodness of God

I have always been a glass-half-full kind of girl. I believe that when we focus on the positive, there's a bigger chance of positive coming out of any situation. I have never understood how people could be dwell on the "empty" all the time. It's hard to maintain negative thoughts. They are heavy and weigh us down.

Psalm 27:13 is clear about this attitude of goodness.

David stood tall, shoulders back, and eyes looking at those who gathered. "I am confident of this: I will see the goodness of the Lord in the land of the living." This verse has three main points: I am confident, goodness of the Lord, and land of the living.

David's posture was important. Displaying confidence encourages people to believe whatever you are saying. I believe these words were intentional to make sure the listeners knew they could trust whatever came next. David talked of goodness; not problems, not fear. Finally, he speaks to the "land of the living." He specifically addresses the people who are alive in Christ, not suffering as non-believers.

It would be too easy to dwell on the bad. I could turn inward, pushing goodness away and focus on the betrayals and what I have lost. I could wax poetic on social media with stories of "woe is me" and "look what was done to me" and "feel bad for me." I am determined NOT to do that.

Tony Robbins, a well-known author and life coach says, "Where focus goes, energy flows. And where energy flows, whatever you're focusing on grows." I believe this 100%.

I've had some good friends comment about my "post-divorce glow-up." I changed my hair and went out of my comfort zone to wear some clothes that were new to me; I occasionally documented the evolution with smiling photos on Facebook. During a trip to Nashville, I took a picture by the famous "angel wings" mural. I posted this picture on Facebook with the caption, "Ready to Fly."

I'm focusing on me. I'm growing. I'm glowing. I'm feeling the goodness of God.

> *"I remain confident of this: I will see the goodness of the Lord in the land of the living."*

Psalm 27:13

Goodness of God

I love Your voice
You have led me through the fire
In darkest night You are close like no other
I've known You as a Father
I've known You as a Friend
And I have lived in the goodness of God, yeah

Cece Winans

(Fielding, Johnson, Cash, Ingram and Jenn Johnson, 2021)

Reflection

When have you clearly seen the goodness of God?

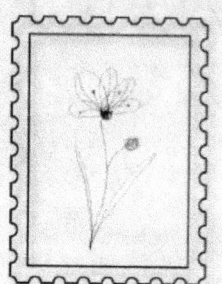

How does focusing on goodness drive your daily outlook?

What practical steps help you keep your focus on God's goodness when negative thoughts try to take over?

What are you grateful for this week?

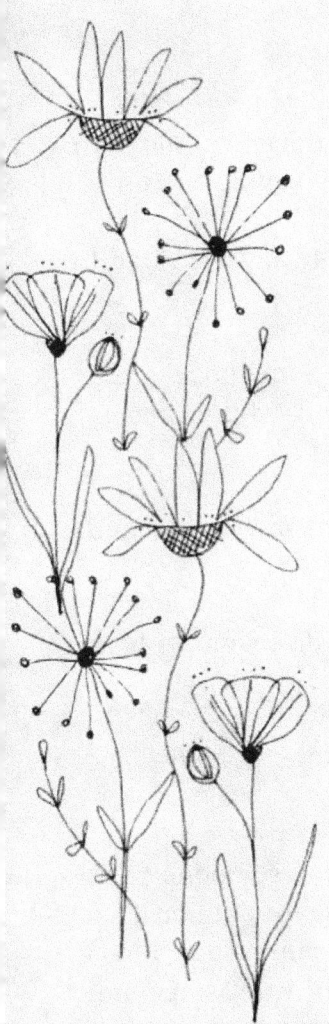

Weekly Prayer

Lord, Thank You for Your unending goodness and for reminding me to stay confident in Your promises. Let my heart reflect Your joy, my words speak hope, and my life shine with the goodness only You provide. Amen.

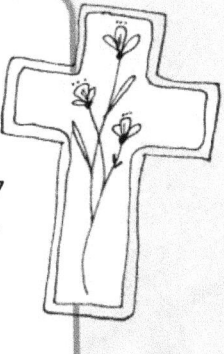

Setting New Goals

I can feel myself growing. I am no longer the person who was afraid to leave and afraid to stay. I'm not the person who thought I should keep it all in.

I have been working on myself through therapy and prayer. I have been reading my morning devotion and digging in deeper to my faith. I have relied on my family and my friends in ways I can never repay.

I want my boys to know I took my decision seriously and I wanted to be a better person at the end of this.

As you can imagine, a new life requires new goals. Some goals are big, and some are quite small. Some require planning while some require patience and persistence.

Proverbs 16:3 reminds me to commit to the Lord whatever I do, and he will establish my plans.

It's time to dream again and set new goals. Where do I want to be in one year? Who do I want in my life?

My first goal is simple but powerful: to pray more intentionally—and with specificity—for the people I love.

In the next year, I'd like to open myself up to meeting someone new. I'm not sure if that would be in the form of someone to date or someone to spend time with in friendship and companionship. I may not know exactly who will be in my life, but I know I want someone with similar beliefs and similar goals, who is walking a path with God.

I'd also like to get involved in something outside of my house and my education business.

New goals will come, but I'll meet them on the path to the future.

For the first time in a while, I'm excited by the future. Even with all the unknowns, I'm excited to see what God has planned for me.

"Commit to the Lord whatever you do,
and He will establish your plans."

The Very Next Thing

Let my very next breath
Breathe out a song of praise to you
With my very next step
Be on a road that was planned by you
Lord, wherever you're leading me
That's where I want to be

Casting Crowns
(Herms, Hall & West, 2016)

Reflection

What new goals do you have in this season?

Which goals excite me most right now?

What does "a fulfilled life" look like to me in this new season?

How are you feeling today?

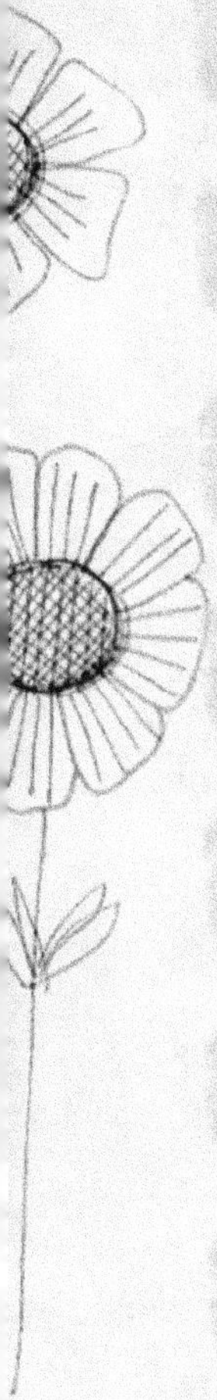

S ☐

M ☐

T ☐

W ☐

T ☐

F ☐

S ☐

Weekly Prayer

Heavenly Father, guide my steps as I set new goals. Help me prepare wisely, trust deeply, and follow where You lead. Let my dreams reflect Your purpose and my actions honor You. Strengthen me to work with patience and faith, knowing You have already prepared the path before me. Amen.

Making Peace with My Past

I was caught in a social media loop the other night, watching video after video. This particular night, while thinking about my upcoming 40th high school reunion, I was watching videos about the 80's and how we were so different from kids today. We rode our bikes without our parents knowing how far we went from home. We played outside for hours, entertaining ourselves and our parents never asked us what we did that day.

We had to rely on "house phones" stuck to the wall in the kitchen or beside our parents' bed; the cords kept us tethered to a particular area. If we missed a phone call we didn't know it, because there were no answering machines or cell phones. We also got away with things that I'm glad weren't documented on social media. We bought teen magazines with actors. We bought 45's and albums.

Looking back was fun and nostalgic. But I wouldn't go back. I think it's where the saying, "been there, done that" has full meaning.

God doesn't want us to look back either. In the story of Lot and his wife, God asks them not to look back. You might recall that when his wife looks back, and she changes to a pillar of salt. She was stuck looking back at the past.

Just as God didn't want Lot and his wife to look back, God doesn't want us to look back. It is no longer our concern. God doesn't want us dwelling on the past. He has a better plan for us.

God wants us focused on the path in front of us because that path is paved with His goodness. God has hope and a future planned for you that doesn't involve looking back. It doesn't involve the "shoulda, woulda, and coulda's" of that life. He wants you to process the past and let it go.

He is in today. He has new mercies and new intentions for your life. The life he has planned is a new adventure with Him by your side. Psalm 37 directs our path forward.

As we delight in Him, he will delight in our path. Knowing our future is taken care of, we remember the past with fondness and look forward with anticipation.

> *"If the Lord delights in a man's way, he makes his steps firm; though you stumble, you will not fall, for the Lord upholds him with his hand."*
>
> Psalm 37:23-24

Your Way's Better

You love every part of me,
even when I was messy
Now I see the heart in Your beauty

Oh Lord, I need You now more than ever
Would You put my heart back together
I searched the world 'til my head hurt
Just to find out Your way's better

Forrest Frank
(Frank & Krsajiic, 2024)

Reflection

What does "making peace with the past" mean to you personally?

When have you found yourself "looking back," and how did it affect your ability to move forward?

What is something God provided that brings you peace?

What are you grateful for this week?

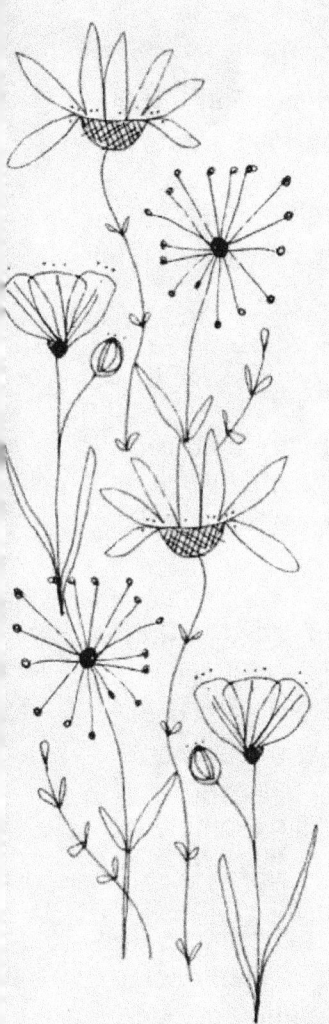

Weekly Prayer

Lord, Thank You for the lessons of my past and the peace You offer in my present. Help me to release what no longer serves me and to trust the path You've prepared ahead. Let my steps be firm in faith and my heart open to new beginnings. Amen.

Just What I Need

I grew up in the church. Between youth group, being an acolyte, singing in choir and helping with vacation bible school, my family was involved throughout the year.

We looked forward to the Easter Brunch, Church Picnic, Fall Bazaar, and the Spaghetti Dinner in the winter. Once a year, my parents' Sunday school class would host a spaghetti dinner. My dad was always in charge of the food. He knows food. You tell him how many people need to be fed, and he can figure out exactly how much food to buy.

Similarly, when the boys were younger, we hosted a soccer camp with friends for 20 boys, ages 12-15. In addition to soccer, we would also have to feed 20 boys, 3 coaches, and 8 helping parents three times a day, so I went to my dad. He helped us make menus, go shopping, and make the meals all week. We fed everyone for 6 days with very little leftover.

When you talk about feeding the masses, we are reminded of the story of the fishes and loaves. So many faithful people had waited all day to hear from Jesus and see him heal the sick. They were tired and hungry and little rations were available. The boy with the basket of meager means supplied the basis for a miracle. The miracle of two fishes and five loaves of bread is a clear example of God providing exactly what we need.

My needs are met in the same way. When I was at my weakest, God was there. Several years ago, I joined a group of ladies online who were a on similar professional path. The goal was to talk business from 10-11am every Monday. We do talk business, but they have been a lifeline in so many ways this past year. They have let me share my journey and have been there unconditionally. I believe God knew that when he brought them into my life all those years ago. He has always been there with just what I needed, and he even placed things in motion before I knew the deeper meaning.

Whether it's a song on the radio, a sermon on Sunday, or a Monday morning ladies' group, he has supplied it all. On days when I felt like I was lacking in faith, He fed me everything I needed.

Knowing my needs will be met, peace comes easily.

"God will generously provide all you need. Then you will always have everything you need, and plenty left over to share with others."

2 Corinthians 9:8

The Lord Will Provide

Look at the flowers in all of their beauty
I don't have to wonder,
You know what You're doing
So why would I worry at all
when You're faithful to supply?
Everything I need, everything I need
My Father has it, my Father has it

Landon Wolffe
& Passion
(Cates, Younker, and Davenport, 2024)

Reflection

Can you recall a time when God provided exactly what you needed, even if it wasn't what you expected?

How do you define the difference between "wants" and "needs" in your spiritual life?

What does it mean to be "nourished in your soul"?

How are you feeling today?

S ☐

M ☐

T ☐

W ☐

T ☐

F ☐

S ☐

Weekly Prayer

Heavenly Father, Thank You for meeting my needs in every season. When I am uncertain or feel empty, remind me that You are my provider and sustainer. Fill my heart with gratitude and trust, so I may share Your blessings freely and reflect Your generosity in all I do. Amen.

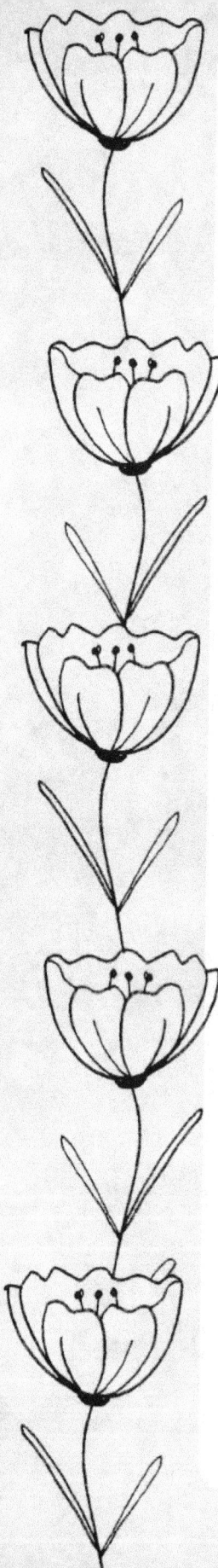

Trusting What Comes Next

At the beginning of this journey, trust was a hard concept for me. I had trusted someone to "have and to hold" and those vows were broken. I had great difficulty truly believing in another person and allowing trust to develop, but I also had difficulty trusting myself.

When I retired, I received a gift certificate for a massage. I had lunch with a friend who begged me to make an appointment with a specific masseur at that spa, "Wait for him. His appointments are always full, but it's worth it. Trust me."

I did. I waited 2 months to get an appointment and from the beginning, my friend was right. I trusted my masseur to make me feel physically better. He learned to read me and could tell by the way I walked in the room if it was my neck or lower back that needed attention. At the beginning of my appointments, he would tease me about trying to keep control. On that table, I have learned to completely relax and give control to someone else. Not only do I know I'll feel better physically, but I also always feel better mentally.

Learning to trust him with my well-being reminded me how carefully trust can be built, and how deeply it can heal when it's rightly placed. It took me a long time to trust him completely, and I've come to realize this habit of being guarded seeped into other parts of life.

Just like my monthly massages, I have come to treasure my relationship with my God. I know He has created my path and chosen wisely for me because He always has my best in mind.

Psalm 37 reminds me that when I *delight in the Lord*, my desires will align with His. God knows the desires of my heart and, better yet, He knows how to fulfill those desires.

He knows what is best for me and I have put my trust in His timing. God can dream bigger dreams for myself than I can, for He is mighty.

Throughout the past year I have learned a lot about myself. As I look ahead, I carry with me the lessons of trust, the peace of God's presence, and the joyful hope that what comes next will be exactly what He has prepared for me.

> *"Delight yourself in the Lord, and He will give you the desires of your heart."*
>
> Psalm 37:4

I Trust Jesus

Who else could stand beside me in the fire?
Who else could part the waters at my feet?
Who else could move the mountains I am facing?
Who else already holds my victory?
I trust Jesus, I trust Jesus
In the storm, in the fight

Matthew West
(Johnson & West, 2023)

Reflection

When have you struggled to trust someone—or even God—and what helped rebuild that trust?

What current situation in your life requires you to trust God's timing instead of your own?

Looking back over the past year, what evidence do you see of God preparing you for what comes next?

What are you grateful for this week?

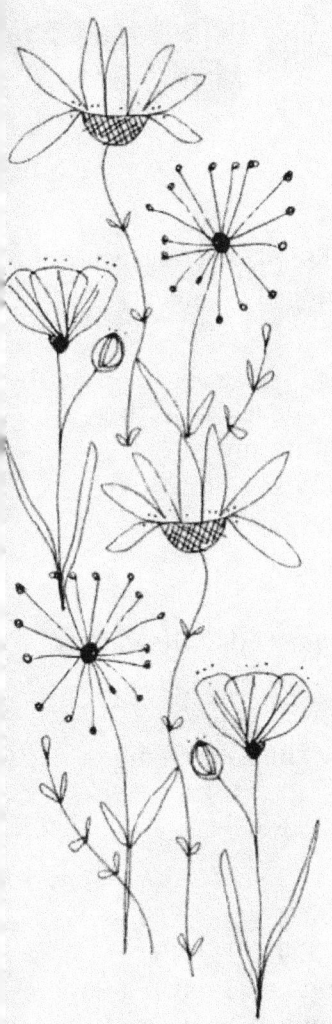

Weekly Prayer

Lord, teach me to trust Your timing and delight in Your plan. When uncertainty clouds my vision, remind me that You hold every detail of my story. Align my heart's desires with Yours, and give me peace as I walk forward, confident that what comes next is chosen by You. Amen.

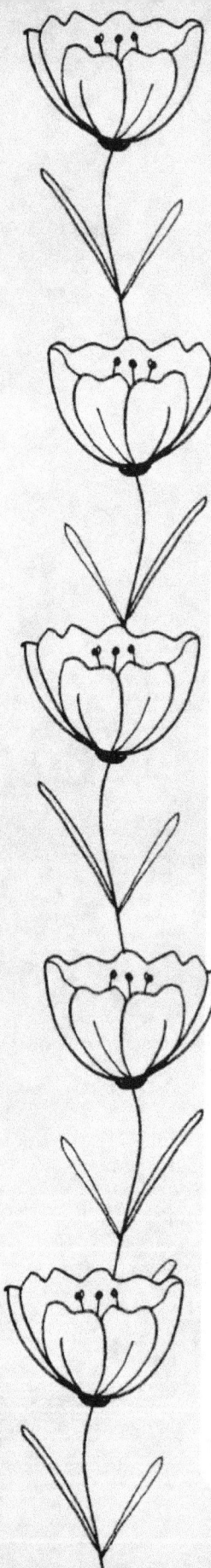

Stronger Than I Knew

I grew up surrounded by love and support, and I'm forever grateful for that foundation. My parents modeled respect and consideration for others, and those lessons have stayed with me. Over time, though, I learned to place a little too much weight on what others might think, often trying to keep the peace instead of sharing my thoughts or living a lie instead of living my truth.

Teddy Roosevelt said, "Comparison is the thief of joy." He was correct. Allowing myself to be measured by someone else's stick was ridiculous. Other people's opinions of me are none of my concern. They didn't walk in my shoes down my path.

As you know by now, I am blessed with friends who have made this path better by a million percent. About six months into my separation my best friend and her husband came to visit. They had taken a red-eye flight, so my friend was napping, and her husband and I were chatting.

"Do you know what my wife told me last night?" He asked. "She said, She's becoming herself again." Man, it really hit me. On one hand, I was sad I had changed and hadn't been honoring who I was for a long time. On the other hand, I was excited to know she saw changes in me and liked what she saw.

I want someone to say, "If she can do it, I can, too."

One of my oldest friends and I were texting the other night. I was telling him I was ready for this part of my life to be done. I felt like I was ready to move on and not be so self-absorbed and in my head anymore. He responded:

You have never been that way in your life. You might feel that way, but it's not the truth. You have been amazingly strong in a bad situation.

I am proud I was strong enough to leave. I am proud I was strong enough to be on my own. I am proud I was strong enough to begin to heal those parts of me that needed it.

I never planned on getting divorced, but it isn't the end of the world. My path led to a new me. I am stronger for having taken it. I am stronger than I knew, but God knew! God knew all along.

"*Do not grieve, for the joy of the Lord is your strength.*"

Nehemiah 8:10

Strong

I can't do this on my own
Lord knows I've tried,
but I'm good at falling down
Thank God You're good at
picking me up off the ground
The world's gonna try to break me
But I know the one who makes me strong

Anne Wilson
(Wilson, Pardo & West, 2024)

Reflection

When have you realized you were stronger than you thought?

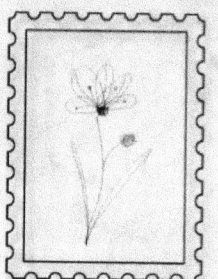

How can we tell the difference between being strong for others and being strong for ourselves?

How can you encourage someone else to discover their own strength through God?

How are you feeling today?

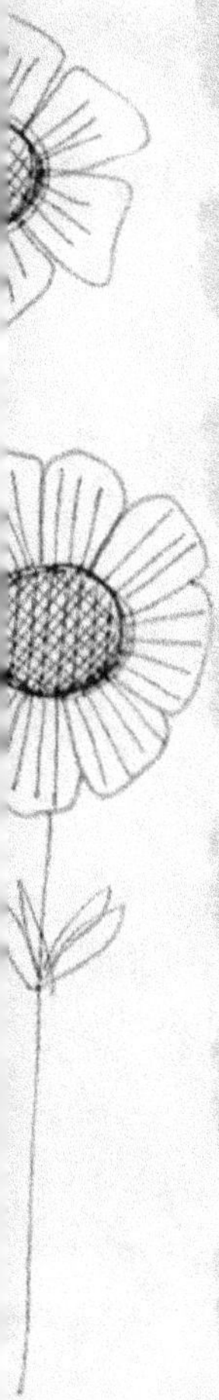

S ☐

M ☐

T ☐

W ☐

T ☐

F ☐

S ☐

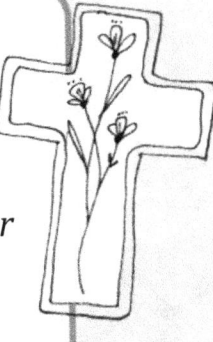

Weekly Prayer

Lord, Thank You for giving me strength even when I doubted it. Remind me that my worth and resilience come from You. May my story inspire others to trust Your power and discover their own strength. Amen.

Braver Than I Knew

Getting divorced is hard; being divorced is not. Getting divorced requires time, money, and lawyers. Nothing goes as smoothly as it should, and timelines are simply suggestions. Being divorced is easy. It's freeing. I could start to live my life.

Although my divorce came as a huge surprise to my parents (and most of the people in my life), they have supported me and encouraged me from the beginning. Like I mentioned in the introduction, my mother has told me so many times this last year that she thought I was brave for leaving and brave for starting over. For a while, it seemed like something she would say every time we hung up the phone.

It has taken me time to realize maybe she was going to say it until I believed it.

Two nights before that all-important meeting with my ex and our lawyers, I had an overwhelming sense of peace blanket me as I laid down for the night. I was suddenly comforted and I audibly said, "Ok God. It's yours. I give you my worry. You are in control." I slept like I hadn't in thirteen months, maybe even in ten years.

As I walked into that meeting, I felt a confidence I hadn't felt before. Maybe for the first time, I felt brave. I wasn't afraid of the meeting or the outcome.

I feel like I'm becoming myself again. I'm embracing my thoughts, my ideas, my beliefs and my dreams again. However, I think I'm a better version of myself. I am not the same person I was. I am bolder. I am more open. I am more aware of my faith. I am okay being alone and that's huge for me.

I am putting myself in the center of my story. I know I'm not done. Just like 2 Corinthians says, "The old is gone, the new is here." I can't wait to see what's next. I have faith that God has a great plan for this new me and I feel excited.

I am proud of myself. Maybe mom had it right all along: I was brave. I was braver than I knew.

"Therefore, if anyone is in Christ,
the new creation has come:
The old has gone, the new is here!"

2 Corinthians 5:17

I Made It

I'm coming out the other side stronger
One foot in front of the other
Hands still raising, Heart still praising
I made it

Through the storms, The hell and high water
I never left the hands of my Father
Lungs still breathing, Thank You, Jesus
I made it

CAIN

(Pardo, N. Cain, M. Cain, Bays & T. Cain, 2025)

Reflection

What old habits or fears do you need to release to fully embrace the "new you"?

How does it feel to "put yourself in the center of your story"?

How can you continue to be brave and move forward while fostering your relationship with God?

What are you grateful for this week?

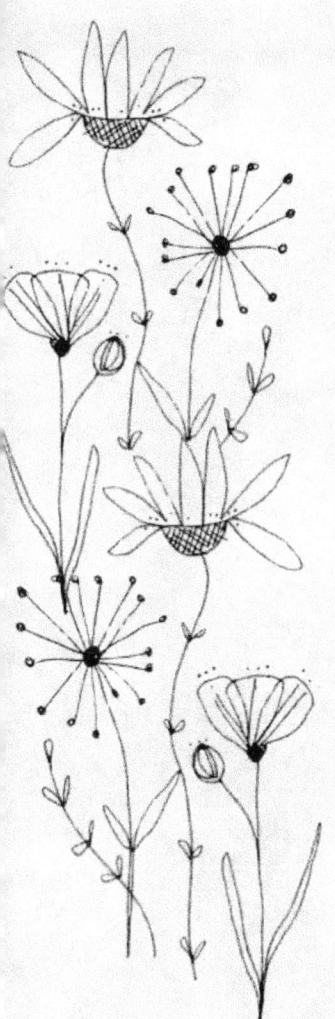

Weekly Prayer

Heavenly Father, Thank You for making me new. Help me let go of the old and embrace the person You are shaping me to be. Fill my heart with courage, faith, and peace as I walk in Your purpose and rediscover the joy of becoming myself again. Amen.

Acknowledgements:

Grant and Austin - thank you for letting me be your mom. I am impressed by you every day. Your grace and compassion through this change in our family has been admirable. Your help and your sincere desire for this to come to fruition has been wonderful.

Katie - thanks for being there for my boys and helping me edit my words.

Mom and Dad - thank you for your encouraging words and continued prayers.

Lisa - thank you for being my best friend, my sister, and my champion. I knew you were there at a moment's notice and your support was unwavering.

Sheryl - more than my cousin, you are my friend, my confidant, and sounding board. Thanks for always having my back.

Heather - thank you for always listening and taking my late-night phone calls. I could count on your presence, even though you were across the country. Our daily chats are still important and I look forward to them everyday.

Susan, Michele, and Stephanie - thanks for all the love, prayers and laughs, even when laughing was hard. Your lunches, visits, and texts kept me going.

Micheal - our daily conversations and check-ins kept me sane more than once. Thank you for being ready with dinner, a drink, or a dip in the pool.

Celia - best therapist ever...and you always will be. You helped me every step of the way and we're just getting started.

Jerry, Bryan, Derek and Michael - you are the best guy friends a girl can have... and you've helped me understand there are great guys out there. I appreciate your strength and your advice.

Tim and Beth and Jim and Leigh Anne - thanks for dinner invitations, packing the U-Haul and fixing my heater. I know I can rely on you guys for anything.

And to all my friends who texted, Marco'd, video chatted, called, sent me messages on social media and prayed for me, I am here because of all of you. You held me up when I was falling, you let me cry when I needed it, and you listened...and listened...and listened (I know I talk a lot).